The European Union After the Crisis

The global financial and economic crisis struck the European Union and its member states with particular force from 2009 onwards. The immediate problem was the knock-on effects of the crisis on each country's public finances. Bank bailouts imposed a massive increase in sovereign debt on member states, while the economic recession unavoidably led to ballooning budget deficits via the usual mechanisms of reduced taxes and increased welfare spending. Subsequently, the Eurozone sovereign debt crisis exposed the hidden weaknesses in the monetary and financial arrangements that had accompanied the launch of the Euro; the severe economic imbalances between member states, rooted in longer-term structural divergences; and the inadequate institutional mechanisms for resolving these difficulties.

The essays in this book originated from an EU-funded international research network on "Systemic Risks, Financial Crises and Credit: The Roots, Dynamics and Consequences of the Sub-Prime Crisis." The contributors explore and evaluate some of the ways in which the institutions and policies of the European Union and its member states have changed in response to the problems brought about by the crisis.

The book was originally published as a special issue of the *Journal of Contemporary European Studies*.

Hugo Radice is a Life Fellow in the School of Politics and International Studies, University of Leeds, where he taught economics and politics from 1978 to 2008. He now works as an independent researcher in political economy, with particular reference to the recent economic crisis.

The European Union After the Crisis

Edited by
Hugo Radice

Routledge
Taylor & Francis Group

LONDON AND NEW YORK

First published 2015 by Routledge

2 Park Square, Milton Park, Abingdon, Oxon OX14 4RN
711 Third Avenue, New York, NY 10017, USA

Routledge is an imprint of the Taylor & Francis Group, an informa business

First issued in paperback 2017

Copyright © 2015 Taylor & Francis

All rights reserved. No part of this book may be reprinted or reproduced or utilised in any form or by any electronic, mechanical, or other means, now known or hereafter invented, including photocopying and recording, or in any information storage or retrieval system, without permission in writing from the publishers.

Notice:
Product or corporate names may be trademarks or registered trademarks, and are used only for identification and explanation without intent to infringe.

British Library Cataloguing in Publication Data
A catalogue record for this book is available from the British Library

ISBN 13: 978-1-138-88973-6 (hbk)
ISBN 13: 978-1-138-08314-1 (pbk)

Typeset in Times New Roman
by codeMantra

Publisher's Note
The publisher accepts responsibility for any inconsistencies that may have arisen during the conversion of this book from journal articles to book chapters, namely the possible inclusion of journal terminology.

Disclaimer
Every effort has been made to contact copyright holders for their permission to reprint material in this book. The publishers would be grateful to hear from any copyright holder who is not here acknowledged and will undertake to rectify any errors or omissions in future editions of this book.

Contents

Citation Information   vii

Introduction
Hugo Radice   1

In memoriam Uwe Becker, 1951–2014   3

1. Variegated Capitalism, das Modell Deutschland, and the Eurozone Crisis
   Bob Jessop   4

2. The Heterogeneity of Capitalism in Crisis-Ridden Europe
   Uwe Becker   17

3. German Ordoliberalism as Agenda Setter for the Euro Crisis:
   Myth Trumps Reality
   Brigitte Young   32

4. Exploring the Keynesian–Ordoliberal Divide. Flexibility and
   Convergence in French and German Leaders' Economic Ideas
   During the Euro-Crisis
   Femke A.W.J. Van Esch   44

5. From the Maastricht Treaty to Post-crisis EMU: The ECB and
   Germany as Drivers of Change
   Arie Krampf   59

6. Enforcing Austerity in Europe: The Structural Deficit as a Policy Target
   Hugo Radice   74

7. The European Social Model after the crisis: the end of a
   functionalist fantasy?
   Charles Dannreuther   85

Index   99

Citation Information

The chapters in this book were originally published in the *Journal of Contemporary European Studies*, volume 22, issue 3 (September 2014). When citing this material, please use the original page numbering for each article, as follows:

Editorial

The European Union After the Crisis
Hugo Radice
Journal of Contemporary European Studies, volume 22, issue 3
(September 2014) pp. 245–246

In Memoriam

In memoriam *Uwe Becker, 1951–2014*
Journal of Contemporary European Studies, volume 22, issue 3
(September 2014) pp. 247

Chapter 1

Variegated Capitalism, das Modell Deutschland, and the Eurozone Crisis
Bob Jessop
Journal of Contemporary European Studies, volume 22, issue 3
(September 2014) pp. 248–260

Chapter 2

The Heterogeneity of Capitalism in Crisis-Ridden Europe
Uwe Becker
Journal of Contemporary European Studies, volume 22, issue 3
(September 2014) pp. 261–275

Chapter 3

German Ordoliberalism as Agenda Setter for the Euro Crisis:
Myth Trumps Reality
Brigitte Young
Journal of Contemporary European Studies, volume 22, issue 3
(September 2014) pp. 276–287

Chapter 4

Exploring the Keynesian–Ordoliberal Divide. Flexibility and Convergence in French and German Leaders' Economic Ideas During the Euro-Crisis
Femke A.W.J. Van Esch
Journal of Contemporary European Studies, volume 22, issue 3
(September 2014) pp. 288–302

Chapter 5

From the Maastricht Treaty to Post-crisis EMU: The ECB and Germany as Drivers of Change
Arie Krampf
Journal of Contemporary European Studies, volume 22, issue 3
(September 2014) pp. 303–317

Chapter 6

Enforcing Austerity in Europe: The Structural Deficit as a Policy Target
Hugo Radice
Journal of Contemporary European Studies, volume 22, issue 3
(September 2014) pp. 318–328

Chapter 7

The European Social Model after the crisis: the end of a functionalist fantasy?
Charles Dannreuther
Journal of Contemporary European Studies, volume 22, issue 3
(September 2014) pp. 329–341

Please direct any queries you may have about the citations to
clsuk.permissions@cengage.com

INTRODUCTION

The European Union After the Crisis

The global financial and economic crisis that followed the collapse of the US sub-prime mortgage market in 2007–2008 struck with particular force at the European Union (EU) and its member states from 2009 onwards. The immediate problem was the knock-on effects of the crisis on their public finances: bank bail-outs imposed a massive increase in sovereign debt on member states, while the economic recession unavoidably led to ballooning budget deficits via the usual mechanisms of reduced tax revenues and increased welfare costs.

Above all, what came to be called the 'European sovereign debt crisis' exposed first the hidden weaknesses in the monetary and financial arrangements that had accompanied the launch of the Euro; second, the severe economic imbalances between member states, rooted in longer term structural divergences; and third, the inadequate institutional mechanisms for resolving these difficulties. As a result, the EU economies, especially their public finances and financial markets, were plunged into turmoil, albeit to very different degrees. The most hard-hit member states were rescued through emergency loans, subject to conditions usually enforced by the European Central Bank (ECB), the European Commission and the International Monetary Fund, collectively dubbed the *troika*. During 2011–2013, a mix of *ad hoc* measures and institutional initiatives gradually restored calm to the financial markets, but at the time of writing (June 2014), the EU economies, and in particular those within the Eurozone, remain becalmed in minimal growth, high unemployment and low bank lending to the business sector. The new institutional architecture aimed at establishing a credible long-term framework for avoiding a repeat of the crisis remains a work in progress.

The papers presented in this special section were all written for a workshop held in Weimar, Germany, on 6–7 December 2012, with the aim of assessing the changes taking place within the political economy of the EU as a result of the crisis. Hosted by the University of Erfurt,[1] the workshop was part of a wide-ranging programme of conferences, networks and publications which took place between 2010 and 2014 under the EU-funded COST-Action ISO902 on the theme of 'Systemic Risks, Financial Crises and Credit: the Roots, Dynamics and Consequences of the Sub-Prime Crisis'.[2] This Action brought together scholars from a wide range of disciplines to research the origins, causes and effects of the financial crisis: key areas of work included the economics, history, culture and politics of financialisation; the development of techniques for modelling decision-making in the crisis; comparative studies of the course of the crisis, notably in eastern Europe; and regulatory responses in relation to financial institutions and markets, in particular in relation to shadow banking.

The Weimar workshop brought together specialists mainly from two of the Action's working groups, WG1 on The New Global Finance and WG3 on Regulatory Responses, with the specific purpose of assessing how the institutions and actors within the EU had reacted to the global financial crisis that had engulfed the world economy in 2008–2009.

Sixteen papers were presented in five panels on the variations in European capitalism and their role in the EU crisis, the role of central banks in the evolution of European finance, the question of social differentiation, the consequences for labour and the wider institutional changes in national and international finance.

The seven papers that follow address in particular three aspects of the EU crisis: the heterogeneity of European capitalisms, the framing of economic policy choices and the effects on particular policy areas. *Bob Jessop* places the analysis of heterogeneity in the context of uneven global and regional development; he then examines the role of German capitalism as a model, and the consequences of growing German hegemony within the evolution of Economic and Monetary Union (EMU) and in the (mis)management of the crisis. *Uwe Becker* collates data on the comparative structure and performance of EU economies, and then examines their institutional development in past decades: he argues for a distinction within the 'embedded' economies between corporatist and patrimonial varieties, the former being both more competitive and better able to execute effective policy changes. *Brigitte Young* recounts the historical evolution of the German model of the Social Market Economy since the Second World War, supposedly founded upon ordoliberal doctrine; she argues that despite the rhetoric of monetary stability and market competition, German policy practice has flexibly accommodated social purposes, and that this more inclusive approach would make a better model for the member states of the EU.

For *Femke Van Esch*, different understandings of how capitalism works influence the direction and effectiveness of changes in economic policies. She uses the empirical method of cognitive mapping to chart the policy responses of four key actors—the political leaders and central bankers of France and Germany—to the unfolding sovereign debt crisis, showing that there was a degree of 'discursive convergence' whose durability remains uncertain. *Arie Krampf* also looks at how far EMU discourses and institutions have really changed in the crisis, but does so by analysing the course of events rather than the discourses of actors. He shows that both the ECB and the German government had to make significant concessions, notably in agreeing a banking union in the context of a reassertion of national fiscal discipline rather than a full fiscal union. This provides the context for *Hugo Radice*'s analysis of the political economy of the EU's 2012 Fiscal Pact: in the overall context of fiscal austerity, the novel deployment of the 'structural deficit' as a policy target subject to legal sanctions raises serious questions about both its practicability and its political consequences for democratic accountability. *Charles Dannreuther* looks at the impact of the crisis in a related but different policy area, that of the European Social Model (ESM), which was originally seen as offsetting the trend towards neoliberalism in the 1990s. He examines the functions of the ESM in integrating the EU's responses to monetary union, globalisation and the financial crisis.

Taken together these seven papers cannot offer a comprehensive guide to the changes taking place in EU policies and institutions, but they provide evidence of the quality and range of the work currently being undertaken across the EU to understand and evaluate these changes.

Hugo Radice

Notes

[1] Thanks are due to Oliver Kessler and his colleagues for their very capable organisation of the workshop.
[2] See http://www.cost.eu/domains_actions/isch/Actions/IS0902

In memoriam Uwe Becker, 1951–2014

This book is dedicated to the memory of one of our authors, Professor Uwe Becker, who sadly passed away in July 2014 shortly after completing the final version of his paper.

Uwe was Associate Professor in the Department of Political Science, University of Amsterdam, and belonged to the Research Group on Political Economy and Transnational Governance. He worked mainly in the fields of comparative politics and political economy, with particular reference to Europe and to the study of varieties of capitalism; recently he had extended his research also to the 'BRICS' economies. During his career he worked as a Visiting Scholar at the European University Institute in Florence, the Wissenschaftszentrum Berlin, the Center for European Studies at Harvard University, Uppsala University, the University of New South Wales and the State University of Rio de Janeiro. His recent works include *Open Varieties of Capitalism: Continuity, Change and Performance* (Palgrave 2009) and (as editor) *The Changing Political Economies of Small West European Countries* (Amsterdam University Press 2011).

An obituary notice has been posted on his department's website at: http://www.uva.nl/en/disciplines/political-science/news/item/uwe-becker-passed-away.html.

Variegated Capitalism, das Modell Deutschland, and the Eurozone Crisis

BOB JESSOP

Lancaster University, UK

ABSTRACT *This article proposes the concept of variegated capitalism as an alternative to the mainstream study of comparative capitalism. It illustrates its plausibility and potential by analysing the halting development of the European Union's initial integration of six broadly complementary 'Rhenish' economies to today's relatively incoherent, crisis-prone variegated capitalist (dis)order. In particular, it focuses on the organization of European economic space in the shadow of* das Modell Deutschland *and its insertion into a world market that is organized in the shadow of neoliberalism. This is then related to the Eurozone crisis, the crisis in Eurozone crisis management and attempts to introduce a new 'union method' of economic governance.*

Theoretical interest in comparative capitalism (CC) and varieties of capitalism (VoC) is not new (for a wide-ranging survey, see Bruff and Ebenau 2014). Most work in this area focuses on categorizing and/or comparing individual cases, types or VoC at local, regional, or national level and largely neglects their structural coupling and dynamic entanglements. The alternative approach developed below proposes instead to analyse the variegated nature of capitalist 'space economies' (on 'space economies', see Sheppard and Barnes 1990). Variegation involves complementarities and tensions among types (varieties) of capitalism in a tendentially singular, yet still incomplete and unevenly integrated, world economy. These complementarities and tensions set limits to the coexistence and co-evolution of varieties within a given space–time envelope marked by specific combinations of spaces of places and flows and of economic cycles and other temporalities. One can then examine whether the interaction of 'compossible' VoC in a more or less complex space economy has benign, neutral, or negative effects on their individual and joint economic performance. This more 'ecological' approach posits that zones of relative stability in a given space economy are typically linked to instabilities elsewhere and/or in the future that derive from differential abilities to displace and/or defer problems, conflicts, contradictions and crisis tendencies. Such differences are related in part to 'vertical' relations between core and periphery (Radice 2000) and to other non-trivial asymmetric capacities to shape the world market. These factors get missed in 'horizontal' comparisons of local, national or regional varieties (Jessop 2012). These asymmetries involve more than relative *economic* efficiency in the allocation of scarce resources to competing uses. For, alongside the market's sometimes not so invisible hand, differential accumulation also depends on the actual or potential exercise of soft power, force and domination. Two examples of asymmetrically interconnected economic spaces that can be studied in terms of variegated capitalism are the pathological co-dependence of the USA and China in a world market context and the increasingly dysfunctional interaction of the neo-mercantilist *Modell Deutschland* and the rest of the Eurozone, especially southern Europe (for details, see Becker and Jäger 2012; Weeks 2014).

European Economic and Political Space(s) in the World Market

The aforementioned emergent properties of a variegated economic space (which cannot be derived from the individual features of its varieties considered in isolation from their co-presence, interdependence and co-evolution) are evident in local, urban, regional and national economies in the European Union (EU), in the changing cross-border, international, supranational and transnational character of European economic and political space, and in the uneven integration over six decades of this heterogeneous space into wider regional, trans-Atlantic and global spaces.

When founded in 1951, the European Coal and Steel Community (ECSC) involved six mostly 'Rhenish' (or 'coordinated market') economies, with the partial exception of Italy. In this sense, the ECSC and, later, the European Economic Community (EEC, established in 1957) initially developed as relatively compatible, indeed, in key respects, already interlocking, variants of regulated capitalism, based on the emerging post-war institutionalized compromises between capital and labour as reflected in social democratic or Christian democratic Keynesian welfare settlements. While the formation of ECSC aimed to promote peaceful coexistence among former belligerents, the Treaty of Rome, which established the EEC, was oriented to integrating the six economies into the circuits of Atlantic Fordism, albeit with tensions between more Atlanticist and more Eurocentric visions of what this should entail (Bieling 2010; Cafruny and Ryner 2007; Milward 1992; van der Pijl 1984).

In particular, this project relied initially on the 'Monnet method' (or community method) of integration. This involved incremental, mainly supranational steps towards positive integration that served to promote Fordist growth dynamics and corresponding modes of regulation in each member state (Ziltener 1999; Bieling 2010). The resulting spillover effects of market integration were expected to deepen political integration on the basis of *regulated* capitalism. While apparently a technocratic process, rival economic and political forces sought to skew it and/or exploit it to their advantage. This method became more problematic with each round of enlargement. For, as new member states with different modes of growth, regulation and welfare regimes joined, heterogeneity increased. Along with Denmark and Eire, which had liberal corporatist economies at the time of accession, 1973 saw the UK join as a liberal market economy (an anomaly behind de Gaulle's earlier veto on UK membership). Its membership helped to relay Anglo-Saxon liberal market influences into the EEC and, from the 1980s, to spread the influence of deregulated international finance into the Continental heartland. Subsequent rounds of enlargement added more kinds of capitalism: peripheral southern Europe (1981, 1986), two more Nordic economies (1995), Central and East European post-socialist economies and the Baltic Republics (2004, 2007), the small island economies of Malta and Cyprus (2004) and, in 2013, Croatia (for one typology of VoC in post-socialist Europe and the former USSR, see Myant and Drahokoupil 2012). Efforts also continue severally and collectively to increase ties with the Middle East and North Africa as part of European economic space.

European economic space illustrates key theoretical and methodological principles of variegated capitalism. These include the dominance within Europe of *Modell Deutschland* as an export-led accumulation regime that, despite significant neoliberal policy adjustments, has remained firmly inside the coordinated market economy camp—partly because of the legacies of Ordoliberalism (on which, see Young, this issue) and partly because of the complex material interdependencies in the German space economy, which includes elements of other Rhenish economies in Northern Europe. For example, alongside its own export strengths, the Netherlands provides important commercial and business services that support *Modell Deutschland*; Austria and the new, post-socialist member states in Central Europe also fit into this accumulation regime. The French economy has other specializations (pharmaceuticals, aerospace, agri-food and fashion goods) and different growth dynamics linked to more dirigiste than neo-corporatist governance arrangements (Schmidt 2002). Moreover, until the Mitterand experiment with 'Keynesianism in one nation' failed and common currency policies developed, France relied more on competitive devaluation than German-style deflation (Aglietta 1982; van der Pijl, Holman, and Raviv, 2011; Stützle 2013). We should also note the important transatlantic links, with the USA (let alone North America as a whole) and the EU constituting a far larger trade and investment bloc than the USA and China (Hamilton and Quinlan 2013). This provides a basis for strong US interest in the forms and effects of crisis management in the Eurozone (AmCham 2012, 2014).

The problematic coexistence of these VoC was aggravated by the uneven impact of the crises of Atlantic Fordism and contrasting responses within and across national models in Europe from the late 1960s through the 1980s. These were the years of 'Eurosclerosis'. However, because crisis has proved a crucial driver of European integration, these developments were far from fatal. Indeed, the accession of the southern European economies (especially Spain) and East and Central European economies enabled the northern member states to moderate their own crises by deepening the regional division of labour within European economic space based on the promotion of peripheral Fordism and the extension of credit. This benefitted the neo-mercantilist German bloc and French industry and also created new investment opportunities for banks and other financial institutions not only from Germany and France but also from Austria, Italy and Sweden. This strategy was spearheaded politically by the Franco-German axis and the European Commission (Stützle 2013). But the unfolding crisis of Fordism also made it harder to rescale demand management and indicative planning from the national to the European level or to establish a tripartite Euro-corporatism to support a European Keynesian welfare state. This created the space for radical neoliberal regime shifts based on a principled rejection of inherited post-war settlements in some member states and more pragmatic neoliberal policy adjustments in others. Combined with the decision announced at the Milan Summit (1985) to adopt a principle of mutual recognition, this further extended their economic and social heterogeneity.

Overall, it became harder for the Monnet method to promote incremental convergence, secure economies of scale through market integration, and harmonize economic and social policy. One response in the fields of economic and, to a lesser extent, social policy was to rely more on negative integration. However, efforts to eliminate restrictions on 'the four freedoms' (the free flow of goods, services, capital, and labour) tended to weaken the coherence of the respective national cores of coordinated market economies and/or to advantage more mobile transnational capital (cf. Scharpf 2010; Stützle 2013; on the neoliberal bias of negative integration, see van Apeldoorn 2002; Altvater and Mahnkopf 2007; Cafruny and Ryner 2007). Negative integration was supplemented from the 1990s by the open method of coordination (OMC), which combines centrally agreed targets with decentralized implementation that allows for economic and political variegation. This said, the OMC has been largely confined to employment, social, health and gender policies and, as labour organizations were weakened through neoliberalism and decisions of the European Court of Justice, it proved harder to defend citizenship and welfare rights through this method of governance. The community method, negative integration and the OMC are individually and jointly ill-suited to the conduct of economic crisis management in a European economic and political space with complex, entangled and variegated crisis dynamics (see below).

Das Deutsche Modell and das Modell Deutschland

The distinction between the VoC/CC and variegated capitalism approaches can be illustrated from the German case. The VoC account regards the 'German model' (*das deutsche Modell*) as the exemplar *par excellence* of a coordinated market economy and examines it as one national variety among others (cf. Hall and Soskice 2001). The variegated capitalism perspective highlights the neo-mercantilist character of the German accumulation regime and its mode of regulation in the context of the German space economy. To distinguish this account, I introduce the notion of *das Modell Deutschland*, which was adopted by the social democratic party (SPD) as a campaign slogan in the 1976 federal election. In this context, 'Modell' connoted a new vision (or projected model) for Germany and an actual institutional configuration (or current model) deemed worthy of emulation elsewhere in Europe (Esser et al., 1979; see also Young, this issue). This dual reference inspired the Constance School of heterodox international political economy to investigate, inter alia, the genesis, specificities and implications of *das Modell Deutschland*, which its scholars linked to Germany's specific insertion into European and world markets, namely, its neo-mercantilist mode of growth (see Simonis 1998). Other schools and scholars in critical international political economy have developed similar analyses.

Das Modell Deutschland as 'current model' is distinguished both by the sheer volume and strong share of exports in GDP compared with other trading giants, such as the USA, Japan and, later, China. Its exports are especially strong in capital goods (notably capital goods for making capital goods) and in diversified, research-intensive, high-quality consumer durables (cf. Porter 1990). Given the limited domestic market in these categories of goods, this export profile has shaped the German state's post-war domestic and foreign economic policy and its general strategy for European integration (Bellofiore, Garibaldo, and Halevi, 2010; Cesaratto and Stirati 2010; Lapavitsas 2012; Posen 2008; Schlupp 1980, Simonis 1998; Streeck 2009). For example, after the initial period of post-war reconstruction, restraining prices and wages was crucial for Germany's capacity to renew its export competitiveness. This domestic deflationary bias has been combined with neo-mercantilist foreign economic policy. In particular, German capital and the German state (initially West Germany, now the reunified state) have sought to shape the governance of the world market, especially in periods of crisis. This is reflected in the German role in regional and international monetary regimes and the problems of managing the deutsche Mark (and, later, the euro) with a view to maintaining both Germany's export competitiveness and the regional and international stability on which its exports depend. Thus, as EU integration has widened and deepened, conditions judged necessary by the German power bloc for export-competitiveness have been imposed on, or otherwise affected, the resilience and potential for growth elsewhere.

Falling productivity and declining profits prompted the Social-Liberal Coalition to pioneer the *Modell Deutschland* strategy (projected model) *avant la lettre* in the early 1970s. It aimed to enhance competitiveness through corporatist arrangements oriented to delivering austerity and 'modernization'. It also sought to prevent economic crisis becoming political crisis by integrating the unions into crisis management so that they would share responsibility for its economic and political costs (Esser 1982; Hübner 1986). By 1981–1982, this crisis-management strategy was no longer effective (for details, see Scharpf 1991) and the resulting crisis of crisis management prepared the ground for a neoliberal turn, *die Wende* (1982–1983), which saw a Christian Democrat-Liberal coalition committed (at least rhetorically) to renewing the social market economy through 'more market, less state'. This *Turn* reflected the exhaustion of the SPD's particular approach to maintaining the German model rather than the collapse of the neo-mercantilist, export-led strategy in general. The new coalition government adapted this strategy to changed conditions rather than trying to *overturn* it. The result was neoliberal policy adjustment within what remained a largely neo-corporatist and neo-mercantilist strategy (Streeck 2009).

The Hartz labour market reforms, which were introduced in 2002–2005 during Schröder's Red-Green coalition (1998–2005) as part of its *Agenda 2010* programme, marked another stage in neoliberal adjustments in *das Modell Deutschland*. In response to slow growth, the coalition stepped up labour market segmentation, wage-restraint and efforts to lower labour costs, including the social wage, to boost export-led growth. Real wage suppression made a significant contribution to the increase in German exports to the EU in the early 2000s, aided by credit-fuelled consumer demand. Greece, Italy, Portugal, and Spain were especially significant sources of demand in this regard (Weeks 2014). It also restrained domestic demand in Germany, contributing to an increasing trade surplus. Paradoxically, then, these neoliberal policy adjustments benefitted the 'Euro-mercantilist' fraction of German capital (Overbeek 2012).

Economic and Monetary Union

The asymmetrical interdependence of the German and other EU economies was reinforced through the formally demanding Stability and Growth Pact. Several sovereign states engaged in deception to meet the convergence criteria and deliberate fudges allowed Italy and Belgium (and subsequently others) to sidestep the national debt-to-GDP hurdle. In addition, austerity and other measures taken by Eurozone members to produce convergence led to structural weaknesses (hidden public debt, cuts in vital infrastructure spending) and reduced expenditure on education, health and welfare to the detriment of long-term competitiveness. More generally, future structural problems were inscribed into the Eurozone at its inception because of tensions among member states that originated in incompatible accumulation regimes, patterns of insertion into European and world markets, modes of regulation and governance capacities. Yet, these tensions were overlooked in the assumptions and operations of the European Central Bank (ECB), which largely derived its policy approach from the *Modell Deutschland* and placed undue faith in an upward economic convergence induced by this further step to market completion.

Originally agreed for political reasons at the Maastricht Summit, Economic and Monetary Union (EMU) was also expected to advance the export-oriented strategy by extending the Deutsche Mark zone (Overbeek 2012). The Euro would be a weaker currency than the DM on its own and thereby enhance the competitiveness of French and German industrial capital, especially when reinforced by direct wage restraint, a reduced social wage and lowered domestic consumption. An expanded, more integrated European economic space would advance the interests of the kind of conglomerates represented in the European Roundtable of Industrialists, which are often connected through interlocks to German capital (van der Pijl, Holman, and Raviv, 2011), so that Europe could challenge the position of the USA, Japan and China and promote the Euro's emergence as a global currency (Overbeek 2012). Reflecting the banking tenets of *Modell Deutschland*, EMU operated on two key principles: first, the ECB may not act as lender of last resort to insolvent banks or indebted states, and, second, sovereign debts may only be discharged by their respective member states (Varoufakis 2013). This led Heise (2005) to argue that Germany's massive impact on the EMU governance justified the term 'Germanic Europe'.

The Stability and Growth Pact and EMU were expected to produce convergence in economic performance by extending (presumptively) efficient free markets. Zones of relative economic stability such as the DM area depend, however, on shifting problems onto zones of instability elsewhere and/or on postponing problems into the future. This is evident in the Eurozone and its crisis. Indeed, the design of EMU was likely to exaggerate imbalances in the medium term rather than reduce them, as the less competitive, peripheral economies could no longer devalue their national currencies and would sooner or later be forced into recession and deflation. There were other grounds for scepticism too. Monetary union was not accompanied by fiscal union and, additionally, there were no credible institutional arrangements to enforce long-term fiscal discipline, compensate for uneven development and economic performance, or coordinate crisis management in a situation where conventional national crisis responses such as devaluation were ruled out. In short, the design of EMU 'removed internal shock absorbers while … magnifying both the probability and magnitude of a future crisis' (Sotiropoulos 2013).

This structural flaw was obscured during the 1990s 'Great Moderation' (linked to US monetary policies and to deflation imported from China) and the initial stimulus in the early 2000s (notably in Southern Europe) that followed the Euro's introduction. Thus the status of the Euro as a world currency and other Eurozone successes were (prematurely) celebrated just 10 years after EMU was introduced (e.g. Pisani-Ferry and Posen 2009). Yet structural incompatibilities and institutional design flaws were already evident before 2009, intensified in 2010–2011 and became acute in 2012. As Yannis Varoufakis, an astute observer of world market dynamics, notes:

> The combination of accumulating profits in the Eurozone's core (due largely to the repression of Germany's wage share) and abundant toxic, or private, money minted by the financial sector (primarily by the City and Wall Street) ensured that no decent

returns could be found in the sluggish Eurozone core itself. So torrents of credit rushed from the surplus to the deficit Eurozone countries in the form of loans and sovereign debt purchases. For 12 years (1997–2008), the capital inflows into the periphery reinforced themselves by strengthening the demand for the core's net exports, part of which was utilised in helping German multinationals globalise beyond the Eurozone (in Eastern Europe, Asia and Latin America). (Varoufakis 2013, 54)

Failure to address the design flaws and the emerging structural problems inherent in a variegated European economic and political space in good times made crisis management harder with the eruption of the North Atlantic Financial Crisis (NAFC), the surfacing and intensification of the Eurozone crisis and the downward spiral of private and sovereign debt–default–deflation dynamics in peripheral economies.

The Eurozone Crisis

The Eurozone crisis is often attributed to the uneven economic performance of national VoC and/or the unsustainable public and sovereign debts of southern member states (the so-called PIIGS plus, latterly, Cyprus). The argument developed above suggests that the crisis can be better understood and explained in terms of the dominance within European economic space of *Modell Deutschland* as a mode of organizing economic relations within *and beyond* German frontiers. In other words, the Eurozone crisis originates in what Dadush and Stancil (2011) term, euphemistically, 'misaligned economic structures and lost competitiveness.' This is reflected in a wide range of micro- and macro-economic divergences in productivity, unit labour costs, competitiveness, trade surplus and deficit positions, and other imbalances, which are often rooted in inherited, but now superseded, economic structures and roles in regional and global divisions of labour (e.g. European Commission 2010; Lapavitsas 2012). These imbalances and disproportions are linked to variations in local, regional and national restructuring and steering abilities; capacities to displace and defer contradictions and crisis tendencies; and the limited resistance of weaker capital fractions and subaltern classes to neoliberal crisis management panaceas. This has affected the form and dynamics of the unfolding financial, economic, political, constitutional and social crises from the moment that the European Single Market project was launched until the present.

In particular, the debt and deficit crises in the Eurozone can be linked to the ecological dominance of *das Modell Deutschland* in European economic and political space and, more immediately, to the labour market and trade policies pursued from the late 1990s onwards (see preceding section). This exacerbated imbalances in macro-economic performance and trade relations that proved unsustainable when the NAFC, which originated in neoliberal market economies, struck the continent in 2008 and produced contagion effects that precipitated debt–default–deflation dynamics that reverberated throughout the Eurozone. With the exception of Greece, public debts and fiscal deficits were not a serious problem—in contrast to mounting private debt that had been unproductively invested in consumption and Ponzi finance of housing bubbles. Nonetheless, the deepening crisis was intensified through market speculation against the perceived weakest links in the Eurozone. Thus, each new shock has highlighted further the structural incoherence within the Eurozone as well as the contagious interconnections with crisis tendencies and crisis dynamics elsewhere in the world market, making it harder to rely on fisco-financial 'extend and pretend' (more politely called 'debt re-profiling') and political 'muddling through'.

Crises of Crisis Management

This has produced crises of crisis management on many scales with open fights among financial officials and government ministers and business lobbies (reflecting broader disputes around capitalist strategies) over how to rescue the Eurozone and the European project and/or to promote the broader world-market interests of transnational capital regardless of particular fallout and blowback effects in Europe. The Eurozone crisis has also intensified the institutional crises in European governance structures and undermined the legitimacy of the European project. Thus, attempts at crisis management are complicated by political crises at different scales, including splits in national and transnational power blocs, representational and legitimacy crises, loss of temporal sovereignty and declining institutional integration.

Initially, the deficit countries under French political leadership called for a collective mechanism to support states in financial difficulties, to create Euro bonds, and to practice comprehensive joint EU management on the basis of the existing treaties. This approach would have obliged the strong export-oriented states to reduce their trade surpluses to lessen the macroeconomic imbalances in the EU. Unsurprisingly, this was opposed by the German government, which represented surplus countries.

In response to mounting problems of crisis management, there have been halting and contested moves to establish a new 'union method' (sometimes designated the 'Merkel method'), to redesign economic governance in the face of the NAFC, its contagion effects in the EU and the specific problems in the Eurozone. Because member states cannot legally use exchange rate adjustments and/or lax domestic fiscal policy to mitigate the deflationary impact of shocks, the Stability and Growth Pact and EMU locked the Eurozone economies into a politics of disinflation and competitive deflation. In May 2010, the European Financial Stability Facility (EFSF) was introduced to provide funding on request to sovereign states in difficulties. The European Financial Stabilisation Mechanism (EFSM) followed in January 2011. The intergovernmental EFSF and EFSM were replaced in September 2012—after negotiations, a treaty amendment and a special Eurozone-only treaty—by a permanent European Stability Mechanism (ESM). This has the power to advance 'bailout' loans in cases where sovereign debt is unsustainable or might become so and/or where governments need to borrow funds to recapitalize distressed banks, conditional in all cases on the recipient state's ratification of the European Fiscal Compact and its signature on a Memorandum of Understanding about fiscal consolidation and other restructuring measures. The Treaty on Stability, Coordination and Governance in the EMU (or Fiscal Compact) was signed by all but two member states in March 2012. When fully implemented, it will constrain national economic sovereignty by setting binding limits (0.5% of GDP) on the structural deficits in the annual budgets of individual member states and thereby constrain national sovereignty. By extending disciplinary neoliberalism, the Fiscal Compact constitutiona-lizes and entrenches the power of capital, limits states' political autonomy and transforms budget-making into a more technocratic process subject to legal sanctions as well as market pressures. The Swiss and German precedents for such a debt brake show that it is hard to measure structural deficits, operate the brake and avoid political manipulation.

As indicated above, the union method is an ad hoc response to the limited treaty powers available to the Commission and/or the ECB to manage the Euro-crisis. In this sense, it corresponds to a state of economic emergency by introducing features of a state of exception (*Ausnahmestaat*) while efforts are made to find ways to restore stability and growth. This has led two commentators to locate these developments in a broader trend towards 'authoritarian neoliberalism' (Bruff 2014) or 'authoritarian constitutionalism' (Oberndorfer 2014) as recent variants of 'authoritarian statism' (Poulantzas 1978). The union method involves concertation, based on their respective competences, among the European Council, Commission and Parliament. This new mode of economic governance subverts the division of competences between member states and the EU that was enshrined in the Maastricht Treaty. It is steered through intergovernmental consensus reached in the shadow of German economic and political power with French support (and cover) after Germany rejected France's efforts to represent deficit countries and Merkel team insisted on the 'no bail-out' clause of the Lisbon Treaty. This locked Germany, France and their allies into preserving the Eurozone 'at all costs' but having to extemporize to achieve this. The Merkel method reproduces and, indeed, reinforces asymmetries between the Eurozone core and periphery, reflecting the size and power of states and their creditor and debtor positions. It also extends 'new constitutionalist' practices (Gill 1998) to budgetary and fiscal policies and, in this context, requires and legitimates the imposition of conditionalities set by the 'Troika', namely, the ECB, European Commission and IMF. This approach to crisis management also created the space for technocratic governance in southern member states, whether through EU and ECB-inspired *coups d'état* (Greece and Italy) or through *de facto* or formal governments of national unity (Spain, Portugal).

In addition, from December 2011, the ECB was released from the ban on acting as a lender of last resort and was authorized to engage in long-term, yield-lowering refinancing operations to prevent any serious bank failure. After the 'Grexit' (Greek Eurozone exit) scare, which led the Troika to offer two further bailout packages (in February and November 2012) to prevent a Greek default, the overall strategic line in crisis management remains consistent with *Modell Deutschland* principles. For example, from September 2012, the ECB implemented a controversial (especially in Germany) outright monetary transactions programme to purchase, albeit only in secondary markets, unlimited amounts of bonds issued by states involved with the EFSF and/or ESM. The crisis in Cyprus led to further crisis measures that included a partial bail-in of bank depositors. In November 2013, the ECB reduced its bank rate to 0.25% as a further boost to recovery.

In general, the Troika has sought to impose the greatest austerity on the weakest member states (Greece, Ireland, Portugal and, latterly, Cyprus, the economic size of which renders all four more vulnerable to such pressures than Spain and Italy), even though this reinforces imbalances and increases debt–deflation–default risks. This reflects the more general paradox that a Eurozone organized in the shadow of a neo-mercantilist *Modell Deutschland* is resorting to recession-led neoliberal restructuring that imposes cuts in direct wages and the social wage as well as privatization and other neoliberal measures in the periphery in order to save distressed banks in core states. This is legitimated by reference to the sovereign debt crises that were created or intensified by public bailouts of financial institutions. Moreover, adopting the terms of neoliberal economic and political discourse, 'painful adjustments' are just as necessary in strong economies, whether in the Eurozone or not, as they are in economies vulnerable to financial collapse and sovereign default.

The continued 'muddling through' seen in the union method is reflected in a chaotic sequence of *ad hoc* emergency measures, taken in response to successive shocks, declining confidence and the debt–default–deflation dynamics that ensure that austerity measures are counter-productive and spread through their 'blowback' effects to a shrinking core of northern economies. On balance, market forces and political pressures discouraged weaker member states from exiting the Eurozone even though partial default and competitive devaluation might have provided some relief from savage austerity measures and facilitate restructuring that did not conform to neoliberal policy prescriptions. In the short and long term, it was also cheaper and less damaging politically for surplus states to do 'whatever is necessary' to preserve the euro. At the same time, 'extend and pretend' policies on private sector debt and use of fiat credit to bail out the private sector created time for private financial entities to reorganize loan portfolios and/or transfer risks to hedge funds, vulture capital and sovereign states. Conversely, mounting resistance in southern Europe and elsewhere against austerity policies has also altered the calculations in the power bloc. This has led to modulated crisis interventions that vary by conjuncture and levels of popular resistance and has prompted further moves towards a post-democratic authoritarian statism.

Conclusions

This article posits the existence of a *fractally variegated capitalism within a tendentially integrating world market* that can be studied at different scales and over different periods. I have tried to make this argument plausible by exploring aspects of European economic space. This is organized in the shadow of neo-mercantilism but has been increasingly integrated into a world market organized in the shadow of a finance-dominated neoliberalism. As Cafruny and Ryner (2008, 60) remarked:

> The EU's aspiration to build a monetary union to promote competitiveness, sustained growth, regional autonomy and social cohesion is self-limiting because the Maastricht design of the EMU is inherently connected to a neo-liberal transnational financial order that displaces socio-economic contradictions from the US to other parts of the world, including Europe. Europe's subordinate participation within this order pre-empts the possibility of resolving structural problems of ... post-Fordist society in a manner consistent with Europe's social and Christian-Democratic accords. Economic stagnation, uneven development, and the widening gap between new forms of governance and social citizenship amplify legitimation problems and political conflicts, with adverse effects on the EU's political ability to mobilize as a counterweight to the US.

While the problems of 'Club Med' economies in the Eurozone are partly related to the impact of *das Modell Deutschland* within European economic and political space, Germany's own room for manoeuvre is limited by the path-dependent effects of its dominance within Europe and the global ecological dominance of neoliberal, finance-dominated accumulation as well as the political struggles over the right approach to crisis management and crisis prevention. In short, divisions in Europe's variegated capitalism are reflected in continuing struggles with important economic and political stakes over how to solve the Eurozone crisis. Past proposals include: a unilateral return to the

Deutsche Mark by Germany; the separation of a strong Northern European bloc centred on Germany from a weaker 'Club Med' bloc, that might have been centred on France; the expulsion or self-exclusion of Greece as the 'weakest link' in the EMU chain or, more broadly, temporary exits from the Eurozone from weaker economies followed by re-entry after restructuring has restored them to robust neoliberal good health; and political union through treaty change. Treaty considerations apart, all these proposals are contraindicated by the dense web of bank loans and credits that creates complex interactions with unintended effects, thanks to the exposure of private and public financial institutions to weak economies and now indebted sovereign states. This creates further exposure to rating agencies and the mighty bond markets, with risks of wider contagion and speculation.

This explains why there are increasing calls for fiscal union to be complemented by economic and even political union. Despite obvious disagreements among member states about the details, key elements of an *institutional* fix for the EU would include: 'a quasi-finance ministry to set and enforce fiscal rules; the ability to raise its own resources; common banking supervision, regulation and deposit insurance; common representation in international institutions; and a mechanism for ensuring the democratic legitimacy of these processes' (Leonard 2011). But such an institutional fix would not magically reconcile the contrasting interests of different fractions of capital, of centre and periphery, of deficit and surplus economies, of capital and workers, of insiders and outsiders, in Europe's variegated capitalism.

Reflecting these fractal complexities within the world market, European economic governance has become a crucial site and stake for contending political forces within *and beyond* the EU. They are seeking to shape its overall strategic direction, specific economic and social policies, and, notably, its approach to crisis management. The EU has been a vector for American neoliberal pressures to redesign the world order as well as for counter-hegemonic attempts to promote an alternative European model. This invites the question whether the Eurozone crisis can be solved through greater economic, fiscal and political integration—the usual response to crises in the EU—or involves a more lasting structural, perhaps terminal, incompossibility. For the moment, it seems that the balance of forces favours neoliberalism *redux*, but structural problems remain and may yet take their revenge.

Acknowledgment

This research has benefitted from discussion with participants in the EU-Cost Action, including Hugo Radice, and from the well-informed comments of two anonymous referees for this journal.

Funding

Research for this article was undertaken during the tenure of a Professorial Fellowship funded by the UK's Economic and Social Research Council (grant number RES-051-27-0303).

References

Aglietta, M. 1982. "World Capitalism in the Eighties." *New Left Review* 136: 5–41.
Altvater, E., and B. Mahnkopf. 2007. *Konkurrenz für das Empire. Die Zukunft der Europäischen Union in der globalisierten Welt* [Competition for Empire. The Future of the European Union in the Globalized World]. Münster: Westfälisches Dampfboot.

AmCham EU. 2012. *Putting Growth Back into Europe. AmCham EU's Strategic Recommendations.* Brussels: American Chamber of Commerce to Europe.

AmCham EU. 2014. *Accelerating Growth and Vitality in the European Economy—AmCham EU 2014–2019 Agenda for Action.* Brussels: American Chamber of Commerce to Europe.

Becker, J., and J. Jäger. 2012. "Integration in Crisis: A Regulationist Perspective on the Interaction of European Varieties of Capitalism." *Competition and Change* 16 (3): 169–187.

Bellofiore, R., F. Garibaldo, and J. Halevi. 2010. "The Great Recession and the Contradictions of European Neomercantilism." *Socialist Register 2011*, 120–146.

Bieling, H. J. 2010. *Die Globalisierungs- und Weltordnungspolitik der Europäischen Union* [The Globalization- and World Order Politics of the European Union]. Wiesbaden: Verlag für Sozialwissenschaften.

Bruff, I. 2014. "The Rise of Authoritarian Neoliberalism." *Rethinking Marxism* 26 (1): 113–129.

Bruff, I., and M. Ebenau. 2014. "Critical Political Economy and the Critique of Comparative Capitalisms Scholarship on Capitalist Diversity." *Capital & Class* 38 (1): 3–15.

Cafruny, A. W., and M. Ryner. 2007. *Europe at Bay: In the Shadow of US Hegemony.* Boulder, CO: Lynne Rienner.

Cafruny, A. W., and M. Ryner. 2008. "Is the SGP Crisis Also the Crisis of the EU?" In *Between Growth and Stability: The Demise and Reform of the European Union's Stability and Growth Pact*, edited by L. S. Talani and B Casey, 60–84. Cheltenham: Edward Elgar.

Cesaratto, S., and A. Stirati. 2010. "Germany and the European and Global Crises." *Journal of International Political Economy* 39 (4): 56–86.

Dadush, U., and B. Stancil. 2011. "Is the Euro Rescue Succeeding?". Accessed January 1, 2014. http://www.voxeu.org/index.php?q=node/6083

Esser, J. 1982. *Gewerkschaften in der Krise* [Trade Unions in the Crisis]. Frankfurt/Main: Suhrkamp.

Esser, J., W. Fach, G. Junne, F. Schlupp, and G. Simonis. 1979. "Das 'Modell Deutschland' und seine Konstruktionsschwächen." [The 'Model Germany' and the Weaknesses in its Construction.] *Leviathan* 1 (1): 1–12.

European Commission. 2010. "The Impact of the Global Crisis on Competitiveness and Current Accounts Divergences in the Euro Area." *Quarterly Report on the Euro Area* 9 (1), (whole issue).

Gill, S. 1998. "European Governance and New Constitutionalism." *New Political Economy* 3 (1): 5–26.

Hall, P. A., and D. Soskice, eds. 2001. *Varieties of Capitalism: The Institutional Foundations of Comparative Advantage.* Oxford: Oxford University Press.

Hamilton, D. S., and J. P. Quinlan. 2013. *The Transatlantic Economy 2013.* Brussels: American Chamber of Commerce to the European Union (AmCham EU).

Heise, A. 2005. "Has Germany Been Europeanised or Has Europe Become (Too) Germanic?" *Intereconomics* 40 (5): 285–291.

Hübner, K. 1986. "'Modell Deutschland': Karriere einer 'ökonomischen Kampfformation'." In *Herrschaft, Krise, Überleben*, edited by H. G. Thien and H. Wienold, 374–393. Münster: Westfälisches Dampfboot.

Jessop, B. 2012. "The World Market, Variegated Capitalism, and the Crisis of European Integration." In *Globalisation and European Integration*, edited by P. Nousios, H. Overbeek, and A. Tsolakis, 91–111. Abingdon: Routledge.

Lapavitsas, C. 2012. *Crisis in the Eurozone.* London: Verso.

Leonard, M. 2011. *Four Scenarios for the Reinvention of Europe.* London: European Council on Foreign Relations.

Milward, A. 1992. *The European Rescue of the National State.* London: Routledge.

Myant, M., and J. Drahokoupil. 2012. "International Integration, Varieties of Capitalism and Resilience to Crisis in Transition Economies." *Europe-Asia Studies* 64 (1): 1–33.

Oberndorfer, L. 2014. "From New Constitutionalism to Authoritarian Constitutionalism." In *Asymmetric Crisis in Europe and Possible Futures*, edited by J. Jäger and E. Springler. Abingdon: Routledge (in press).

Overbeek, H. 2012. "Sovereign Debt Crisis in Euroland: Root Causes and Implications for European Integration." *International Spectator* 47 (1): 30–48.

Pisani-Ferry, J., and A. S. Posen, eds. 2009. *The Euro at Ten: The Next Global Currency?* Washington, DC and Brussels: Peterson Institute for Internal Economics and Bruegel.

Porter, M. E. 1990. *The Competitive Advantage of Nations.* Basingstoke: Macmillan.

Posen, A. S. 2008. "Exportweltmeister—So What? Better Goals for German Foreign Economic Policy." In *Economic Policy Prospects for Germany and Europe*, edited by R. Schettkaut and J. Langkau, 119–143. Abingdon: Routledge.

Poulantzas, N. 1978. *State, Power, Socialism*. London: Verso.

Radice, H. 2000. "Globalization and National Capitalisms: Theorizing Convergence and Differentiation." *Review of International Political Economy* 7 (4): 719–742.

Scharpf, F. W. 1991. *Crisis and Choice in European Social Democracy*. Ithaca, NY: Cornell University Press.

Scharpf, F. W. 2010. "The Asymmetry of European Integration. Or: Why the EU Cannot Be a Social Market Economy." *Socio-Economic Review* 8: 211–250.

Schlupp, F. 1980. "Modell Deutschland and the International Division of Labour." In *The Foreign Policy of West Germany*, edited by E. Krippendorff and V. Rittberger, 33–100. London: Sage.

Schmidt, V. A. 2002. *The Futures of European Capitalism*. Oxford: Oxford University Press.

Sheppard, E. S., and T. J. Barnes. 1990. *The Capitalist Space Economy*. London: Unwin Hyman.

Simonis, G. 1998. "Das Modell Deutschland." In *Deutschland nach der Wende. Neue Politikstrukturen* [Germany after the Turn. New Political Structures], edited by G. Simonis, 257–284. Opladen: Leske+Budrich.

Sotiropoulos, D. 2013. "Addressing the Rationality of 'Irrational' European Responses to the Crisis." Paper presented at the 8th Pan–European conference on International Relations, Warsaw, September 18–21.

Streeck, W. 2009. *Re-forming Capitalism. Institutional Change in the German Political Economy*. Oxford: Oxford University Press.

Stützle, I. 2013. *Austerität als politisches Projekt. Von der monetären Integration Europas zur Eurokrise* [Austerity as a Political Project. From the Monetary Integration of Europe to the Eurocrisis]. Münster: Westfälisches Dampfboot.

van Apeldoorn, B. 2002. *Transnational Capitalism and the Struggle over European Integration*. London: Routledge.

van der Pijl, K. 1984. *The Making of the Atlantic Ruling Class*. London: Verso.

van der Pijl, K., O. Holman, and O. Raviv. 2011. "The Resurgence of German Capital in Europe." *Review of International Political Economy* 18 (3): 384–408.

Varoufakis, Y. 2013. "From Contagion to Incoherence: Towards a Model of the Unfolding Eurozone Crisis." *Contributions to Political Economy* 32: 51–71.

Weeks, J. 2014. "Euro Crises and Euro Scams: Trade Not Debt and Deficits Tell the Tale." *Review of Political Economy* 26 (2): 171–189.

Ziltener, P. 1999. *Strukturwandel der europäischen Integration. Die Europäische Union und die Veränderung von Staatlichkeit* [Structural Change in European Integration. The European Union and the Transformation of Statehood]. Münster: Westfälisches Dampfboot.

The Heterogeneity of Capitalism in Crisis-Ridden Europe

UWE BECKER

University of Amsterdam, The Netherlands

ABSTRACT *To get a realist picture of the economic crisis in Europe, we need to know the heterogeneity of European capitalism. Differences in terms of competitiveness and institutions are huge. With the crisis as point of departure, I will outline this heterogeneity. First, I describe the comparative (dis-)advantages of selected EU-member states. The differences are big, particularly in terms of economic specialisation and innovation capacity—aspects getting little attention in the standard literature. In the second part, the paper concentrates on institutional development in the past decades. To identify gradual differences and change, I distinguish ideal-typical from empirical capitalisms, which are located in the field between the types. Based on state–economy and capital–labour relationships as criteria, my types are liberal and embedded capitalism of which the latter is split into statist, patrimonial and corporatist types. Data from the Index of Economic Freedom, the OECD and the World Bank are rough indicators to locate the cases, but show that the strongly corporatist capitalisms in the Nordic countries are highly competitive, while competitiveness and the capacity adequately to act declines the more patrimonial capitalism is, as in the Mediterranean countries.*

The crisis of the economy in the EU, which was triggered by the financial melt-down in 2008, by now has lasted for several years, notably in the southern member states. One of the reasons for this divergence is that the process of economic convergence did not proceed as was expected with the introduction of the Euro in most member states. Put simply, in terms of competitiveness, the North is still considerably stronger than the South. And with the institutionalisation of the EMU and the 'one-size-fits-all' policy, Eurozone member states lost their capacity individually to adapt to changing circumstances by monetary policy (Scharpf 2013). Based on loans with interest rates lower than inflation, southern countries such as Greece and Spain featured high growth rates after the introduction of the Euro, but could no longer react by exchange-rate depreciation or other protectionist measures when they ran into trouble after 2008 (see also Price 2013). The liberalisation of the European market did deliberately not provide for this option, and until 2008 the financial markets, which could have corrected excessive lending by raising interest rates for less competitive member states of the Eurozone, had been sleepy.

The crisis, which is the point of departure but not the subject of this paper, is accompanied by a debate between protagonists of austerity and authors who prefer a Keynesian remedy. A remarkable aspect is that the discussion takes place on a very abstract and general level, the level where the rationally choosing *homo economicus* is active. There is much ado about unit labour costs, rent levels, productivity, spending and consumption, but not about the product specialisation where labour costs and productivity arise.

Would a spending programme help the most affected countries? Would the Greeks and Portuguese build more houses—as the Irish and Spanish did up to 2008, when loans were cheap—and consume more of the vegetables they produce when they would receive an income boost, or would they buy more German cars and Asian-made cell phones and by doing this enlarge their negative current accounts? Or would they, given their indebtedness, save the money? When cheap money was available in the years up to 2008, the current account deficits of Spain, Portugal and Greece surged before they went down again (see Table 1) because interest rates climbed and austerity measures started.

Or do we have to locate the main cause of the crisis primarily in the northern countries, particularly Germany, with their current account surpluses and relatively low wage levels? Is competition first of all price competition, and should we therefore assume that the Mediterranean countries would take over parts of the production of high-quality machinery and cars when wages would be raised in the northern EU countries and make their goods more expensive? Would current accounts become more balanced?

These questions cannot be answered by only considering abstract entities such as wages or unit labour costs on which prominent authors in the discussion concentrate (for example Jones 2010; De Grauwe 2011; Scharpf 2013). Therefore, I look at the differences between a number of European political economies in terms of economic structure, specialisation and innovation capacity. Thereafter, I want to inventory, as far as possible quantitatively, their institutional and relevant socio-cultural differences which inform us about the policy-makers' capacity to get things done. Knowledge of these differences is crucial for a more profound discussion as well as for reasonable policy choices. The selected countries,

Table 1. Employment by sector as % of total employment; exports as % of GDP; current account balance as % of GDP

	Agriculture	Industry	Services	Exports	Current account balance		
	2007			2010	2003	2008	2010
Estonia	–	–	–	78	− 11.3	− 9.6	3.5
Finland	4.6	25.8	69.7	39	5.2	2.9	2.9
France	3.2	22.6	74.2	26	0.8	− 2.0	− 2.1
Germany	2.3	30.0	67.7	46	1.9	6.2	5.6
Greece	11.6	22.4	66.1	21	− 6.6	− 14.7	− 10.4
Ireland	5.4	27.5	67.0	91	0.0	− 5.6	− 0.7
Italy	4.0	30.5	65.5	27	− 1.3	− 2.9	− 3.2
Netherlands	3.0	19.1	77.9	78	5.5	4.4	7.6
Portugal	11.7	30.7	57.6	31	− 6.5	− 12.6	− 9.7
Slovakia	4.2	39.4	56.4	81	− 6.0	− 5.9	− 4.0
Spain	4.6	29.4	66.0	30	− 3.5	− 9.6	− 4.5
Sweden	2.2	21.6	76.1	50	7.0	8.8	6.3
UK	1.4	22.4	76.3	29	− 1.6	− 1.6	− 2.5

Sources: OECD (2009, 30f) and OECD (2011).

representing eastern, southern and northern Europe, are Estonia, Finland, France, Germany, Greece, Italy, the Netherlands, Portugal, Slovakia, Spain plus, though not in the Eurozone, Sweden and the UK.

Some Structural Economic Features

Let us start with the employment structures. A remarkable feature is that two of the particularly crisis-ridden economies—Greece and Portugal—still have more than 11% of the working population employed in agriculture and fishery (Table 1). Levels of 3% or less tend to be normal in modern economies. Worth mentioning are furthermore the relative high percentages of industrial employment in Germany, Italy, Spain and notably Slovakia, while these percentages are low in Sweden, France, the UK, Greece and the Netherlands. As a consequence, there are also huge national differences in the size of the service sector.

Table 1 furthermore informs about exports as related to GDP. Ireland, Estonia and the Netherlands have a remarkably high export level. In such cases, one has to take into account the degree of re-exports, however. The Netherlands with the huge Schiphol airport and Rotterdam harbour is a classic transit country for goods coming from overseas. Estonia and Ireland, by contrast, are highly involved in the global division of labour where parts of goods are produced in different countries and shipped back and forth. Also remarkable is the low export level of the southern crisis countries. Their integration in the world market is only modest.

Table 2 provides detailed information on export specialisation. Apart from vehicles and pharmaceuticals, it presents clusters of branches/goods that the *Intracen* database mentions separately. The table not only lists big branches with comparative advantages—such as Finnish furniture or German car industry—but also those bigger branches with import surpluses. Which are the data worth mentioning? Probably that Estonia is such a big exporter of oil and basic materials, which is because the country is a big producer of oil shale. Greece is strong in services (transport, tourism) and relatively strong in bauxite mining and, as a consequence, aluminium production ('other metals'). Ireland is a top exporter of pharmaceuticals, while Slovakia and Spain received much FDI in the car industry and are big vehicle exporters since then. Slovakia is also strong in electronics, and Portugal might surprise with a slight surplus in this branch, though it is particularly these branches where the division of labour and the level of outsourcing of partial production processes are high.

Finally, it is perhaps a surprise that in relative terms, Greece and the Netherlands are the biggest agricultural exporters. Important differences, however, are that Dutch exports as percentage of GDP are much higher than Greek exports and that Dutch agricultural production is highly developed (though polluting) while the Greek counterpart is very labour-intensive. Generally, Greek export specialisations exhibit, much more than those of Portugal and Spain, let alone Italy, the profile of a less-developed economy. One has to add, however, that Greek exports are small and that services, particularly in transport (shipping is worth mentioning), account for more than half of them. Finally, Ireland—out of the EFSF programme since 8 December 2013—is strong in modern industries and shows itself to be a relatively modern economy (see also Table 3) that in terms of competitiveness is ahead of the Mediterranean economies.

Main findings of Table 2 are confirmed by data on innovation in Table 3. It puts together data on structural conditions for innovation, R&D spending, efforts to innovation at the

Table 2. Export specialisation in selected EU countries in 2010, ≥4% of 'main goods' (exclusive services; in brackets: exports minus imports) and services as % of total exports (column 10)

	Oil, gas, basic materials	Electrical, electronic, optical	Agricultural, fishery	Machinery, tools	Vehicles	Steel, other metals and plastics	Pharmaceuticals	Furthermore worth mentioning[a]	Services; % of total exports
Est	28.3 (−4.1)	18.0 (+0.4)	7.0 (+0.6)	6.8 (−0.7)	4.8 (−0.6)	6.8 (−1.3)	Low	F 6.9 (+3.0)	27.6
Fin	11.4 (−8.5)	15.1 (+2.6)	Low	13.5 (+2.3)	Low	10.3 (−1.9)	Low	F 14.5 (+12)	25.2
F	6.6 (−8.0)	11.8 (−0.8)	9.9 (+4.2)	11.9 (+0.3)	9.2 (−0.2)	8.4 (+0.5)	6.4 (+2.4)	A 9.1 (+5.0)	21.6
Ger	9.2 (−10.1)	14.6 (+0.4)	Low	17.6 (+5.4)	15.7 (+8.6)	8.5 (+0.3)	5.3 (+0.9)	C 6.1 (+0.5)	15.1
Gr	14.4 (−9.9)	5.8 (−2.6)	25.5 (+17.4)	4.6 (−1.9)	Low	16.7 (+9.3)	6.2 (−1.0)	T 5.0 (−15.8)	61.9
Ire	5.6 (−14.5)	14.3 (+3.2)	Low	7.6 (−3.2)	Low	Low	26.1 (+19.9)	C 25.6 (+18.5)	46.5
It	7.4 (−14.4)	8.8 (−2.9)	7.8 (+1.2)	20.1 (+11.3)	7.2 (−1.3)	9.1 (−1.5)	Low	T 8.0 (+2.4)	17.8
NL	24.8 (−4.4)	12.7 (−1.2)	17.5 (+9.1)	14.8 (+0.2)	Low	8.0 (+2.2)	Low	C 7.1 (+1.8)	18.9
Por	10.3 (−5.9)	9.9 (−0.1)	8.7 (−1.0)	6.4 (−2.9)	11.8 (+0.1)	9.1 (−0.2)	Low	F 5.9 (+2.6)	32.0
Sk	4.9 (−7.8)	25.4 (+3.6)	Low	10.1 (−0.4)	20.4 (+8.8)	12.0 (+1.5)	Low	None	8.3
Sp	8.3 (−11.1)	7.3 (−3.4)	10.1 (+3.1)	7.7 (−1.5)	17.5 (+7.8)	10.2 (+2.2)	4.5 (+0.1)	T 4.9 (−1.3)	32.7
S	17.4 (−0.6)	16.7 (+0.5)	Low	14.8 (+1.2)	8.5 (−1.1)	10.2 (+0.9)	5.4 (+2.7)	F 8.6 (+5.5)	28.5
UK	19.1 (+0.7)	11.6 (−0.8)	Low	14.7 (+2.3)	9.2 (−0.3)	4.1 (+1.4)	8.1 (+4.0)	C 5.2 (+0.6)	35.6

Sources: Intracen (2012) (main goods); WTO (2012).
[a] A = aircraft; C = chemicals; F = furniture; T = textiles.

Table 3. Country groups of innovation capacity in 2008 and 2012 on a scale from 0 to 1

Innovation leaders	Sweden ('08: 0.73; '12: 0.75), Germany (0.68; 0.72), Finland (0.66; 0.68)
Innovation followers	Netherlands (0.58; 0.65), UK (0.58; 0.62), Ireland (0.55; 0.58), France 0.52; (0.54), Estonia (0.42; 0.5)
Moderate innovators	Italy (0.44; 0.45), Spain (0.39; 0.41), Portugal (0.38; 0.41), Greece (0.36; 0.34), Slovakia (0.29; 0.34)

Source: European Commission (2013, 5, 74).

firm level, added value in innovative sectors and results in terms of successful know-how. Finland, Germany and Sweden with their strong export profile also are, according to the *European Innovation Scoreboard*, 'innovation leaders'. Sweden is top and indicates that competitiveness is the fundament of its (still) generous welfare system. France, Ireland, the Netherlands, the UK as well as Estonia are named followers in this system, while the remaining economies of our sample are called moderate innovators. This classification confirms the competitiveness gap between a strong North and a weaker South with emerging eastern Europe (except Estonia) also at the lower end. Between 2008 and 2012, the gap has not been narrowed.

Ideal Types, Empirical Cases and Indicators for Localising Cases

Now we move to institutional diversity. Most national capitalisms differ gradually from each other and their institutional change is also gradual. To get a view of this diversity by grades, we need to work with a typology. With numerous empirical cases, a typology brings down the number of alternatives, and for this purpose has to consist of only a limited number of types. In comparative research, typologies are tools to bring order and simplicity into the analysis of a complex reality. They do not explain anything. At least two sorts of typologies exist: those that classify or label cases as belonging to certain types (as in 'UK capitalism is liberal') and those that distinguish ideal types and empirical cases where the latter are located in the field between the former.

If one wants to catch gradual differences and gradual change, then classifications are a dead end street, because by this method differences and change can only be conceived in absolute terms. The mainstream on capitalist varieties (VoC theory) is doing this: National political economies belong either to type A (liberal) or to type B (coordinated) and change only takes place from A to B or vice versa. Ultimately, this is a static approach, and as a rule the distinction between LME cases ('LMEs') and CME cases ('CMEs') is quite arbitrary.

Therefore, we need the distinction between types as ideal types and empirical cases. Ideal types are empirically based constructions of idealised realities. Their construction depends on someone's comparative knowledge of various cases. Cases are entities such as countries, historical stages or, as in this text, national political economies (they are national by their economic specialisation and their specific institutional mix). They are not built by design and *never represent* ideal types; purely liberal capitalism does not exist, even the USA is only highly liberal. Cases *approximate* types; the latter are fixed entities, the former located between them (Becker 2009, 44–50, 2011; cf. Crouch 2005, 61f).

The criteria of a typology have to point to *fundamental economic features*. Resembling those of Schmidt (2002, 107f) and covering most institutional components, the VoC mainstream identifies my criteria as (a) *the relation between politics and economy* (including employment protection, the welfare system, product-market regulation, privatisation/nationalisation, wage regulation and the character of economic policy) and (b) *the relationship between capital and labour* (involving industrial relations as well as those between management and employees, firms and investors and stakeholders and shareholders). The very concept of *political economy* suggests the choice of the first criterion, and the capital–labour relation is the central, and conflictual, cleavage of capitalism.

Which types should be constructed by these criteria? Since capitalism is a market economy, a liberal type is basic. Being very parsimonious, a simple dichotomy then is liberal versus coordinated as in the mainstream on capitalist varieties or, following Polanyi (1957), liberal versus embedded capitalism, which is a more elastic term. A dichotomy obscures fundamental differences, however. Highly corporatist Norway, highly statist France and highly clientelist Greece would all have to be located on the axis between liberal and embedded. This works when one wants to determine the extent of liberal capitalism, but to take into account the fundamental differences just mentioned we need to differentiate embeddedness.

Hall and Soskice (2001) already discussed a 'mixed type', which logically does not make sense, however, because cases but not types are mixed. And geographically defined types such as 'nordic' and 'mediterranean' become problematical when change has to be identified. Worth considering are the typologies of Schmidt (2002) distinguishing market, state and managed (or corporatist) capitalism and Boyer (2005) who mentions market-based, social-democratic, statist and (pointing to an empirical basis in East Asia not relevant here) meso-corporatist types. I follow them roughly by splitting embeddedness into statism and corporatism and add, in the tradition of Weber (1972), a patrimonial type which has to cover the reality of clientelist state–economy relations. Increasing the number of types to four still meets the parsimony criterion. Briefly circumscribed:

(1) In the *liberal type,* the market governs all aspects of the economy and politics unrestrictedly facilitates private property and the market. State interventionism is limited and industrial relations are individualised.

(2) In the *statist type,* the market is restricted by political regulation to determine the course of the economy. State-owned firms might be prominent. A hierarchical organisation of firms fits best, and formal labour organisations are weak.

(3) The *corporatist type* defines institutionalised capital–labour cooperation. Peak organisations and the state negotiate on long-term socio-economic targets. Commitment to pragmatism and the common good, however contested, underlies corporatism.

(4) The *patrimonial type* points to patron–client relationships between state and economy. It is related to corruption and involves a specific interaction pattern between political centre, local politicians and business firms exhibiting favouritism in the distribution of legal permits, government grants and special tax breaks. Ideal-typically, patrimonialism features a weak legal system: not universal rules but personal connections are decisive.

Where in the space between these ideal types do we have to locate the selected political economies? First I want to answer this question with respect to the dichotomy of liberal and embedded capitalism, and thereafter I will turn—rather cursorily because of the weaker data situation—to the levels of statism, patrimonialism and corporatism. In both steps, I will specify the institutional change that occurred between 1998 and 2008, the years for which the best data-sets are available—including employment protection data. Indicators to look for are, for example, the levels of: state ownership of production assets, market capitalisation, public expenditures, price control, Product Market Regulation (PMR), wage bargaining coverage, employment protection and welfare benefits, employee influence within firms, the freedom of trade, investment and establishing a company as well as the level of capital–labour collaboration and corruption (for details see Becker 2013).

It has to be stressed that 'some precision' of measurement is all that is possible here. We are dealing here with the quantification of quality, and the indicators are often 'soft' survey-based data. Sometimes data are lacking and the available ones only crudely approximate the relevant reality, and sometimes data are to some degree 'subjective' and comparisons lopsided. And do all indicators have the same weight? If not, what is the logic of differentiation? Quantification of quality and weighting every indicator is not possible without some degree of arbitrariness, and therefore not without violating the principle of precision.

The available data roughly cover the indicators just mentioned. They are based on surveys and law texts and collected by the Heritage Foundation in collaboration with the Wall Street Journal (*Index of Economic Freedom,* IEF), the OECD (indices of *PMR* and *Employment Protection Legislation,* EPL) and the World Bank (*Worldwide Governance Indicators,* WGI). These organisations have a liberal bias (the IEF scores for high public spending, for example, are very low), but this does not distort any use of the data. The PMR, EPL and IEF indices reveal a dichotomous structure of market versus political regulation with the IEF adding corruption as third dimension. They are suitable for the differentiation between liberal and embedded capitalism. The WGI data measure effective political, judicial regulation and control of corruption. They can be used to distinguish statism and patrimonialism. Recent data on corporatism covering the selected countries are lacking, however. We have to rely on older and incomplete data, therefore, and cannot present more than rough estimates.

Movements Between Embedded and Liberal Capitalism

Let us start with the *Index of Economic Freedom.* It is the broadest index and it works with a scale of 0–100 of 'freedom'/liberalism. Thereafter, we turn to the OECD's PMR and EPL indices, where 0 is the highest liberal value and 6 the lowest. The scores will be converted into the 0–100 scale.

The IEF is composed of 10 single indicators, each with the same weight: (1) business freedom, (2) trade freedom, (3) fiscal freedom (taxation level), (4) government spending, (5) monetary freedom (how much inflation and political price distortion?), (6) investment freedom, (7) financial freedom, (8) property rights (legal framework and judicial protection of private property), (9) freedom from corruption and (10) labour freedom. Labour data do not exist for the years before 2008, and monetary freedom is too much bounded to a certain idea of the causes of inflation and price distortion. I will include neither these indicators nor property rights, which are an aspect of the rule of law and accounted for in the WGI. Attempting to soften the liberal bias of the IEF, I have put together freedom of trade and investment, because separately they would count too much as compared to, for example, business or labour freedom. I also merged the related fiscal freedom and government spending because taxation and public spending are highly related. So, the selected indicators of the IEF are: *Business freedom* (level of regulation of business operations); *trade freedom* (level of trade restrictions) put together with investment freedom (easiness to invest; level of equality of opportunity to invest); *fiscal freedom* (the taxation level) put together with government spending; *financial freedom* (the business freedom of the financial sector) and *freedom from corruption*. Table 4 shows their scores.

Striking features of Table 4 are not only the relatively low average scores of Greece, Italy and Portugal,[1] but also the high liberalisation jump of Finland, Ireland, the Netherlands, Slovakia, Spain and Sweden—in the first and last cases despite the low score in fiscal freedom (taxation) and public spending (here the liberal Heritage Foundation clearly 'punishes' social democracy). By contrast, according to these data in Germany, Greece and Italy, as well as in the already highly liberal Estonia and UK, liberalisation between 1998 and 2008 was modest.

To see whether the OECD's scores for *PMR* and *EPL* confirm or correct the IEF data, we have to look at Table 5. EPL is a monolithic indicator. It informs about the commodification of labour, and in this text it is the main indicator of the capital–labour relation. PMR is more complex and consists of many sub-indicators. The first layer contains 'state control', 'barriers of entrepreneurship' and 'barriers to trade and investment', which all count for one-third in the overall PMR index. While the last two sub-indicators are also part of the IEF and might balance the IEF data, state control is specific to the PMR index. Sub-indicators of state control are public ownership and 'involvement in business operations', which at a lower level are sub-divided into 'scope of public enterprise' and price control (Wolf et al. 2010, 8).

Table 4. Index of economic freedom, 1998 and 2008; seven indicators plus average

	Average[a]		Business		Average of fiscal F & public spending		Financial		Average investment & trade F		Freedom from corruption	
	1998	2008	1998	2008	1998	2008	1998	2008	1998	2008	1998	2008
EE	74.4	78.9	85	85.3	63.7	74.0	67	80	86.5	88.0	70	67
FI	60.4	79.2	70	95.5	19.3	46.7	50	80	71.6	78.0	91	96
F	58.5	66.9	85	88.0	23.4	32.2	50	70	63.9	70.5	70	74
Ger	67.0	71.8	55	89.9	32.3	46.2	90	60	74.7	83.0	83	80
GR	55.3	58.3	70	70.4	52.8	61.7	30	50	73.9	65.5	50	44
IR	68.0	81.6	85	93.0	42.3	63.0	50	90	85.5	88.0	77	74
IT	55.4	60.7	70	77.0	28.9	41.8	70	60	73.9	75.5	34	49
NL	69.9	79.5	70	88.0	28.5	44.7	90	90	73.9	88.0	87	87
PT	61.7	64.3	70	80.5	49.6	47.0	50	50	73.9	78.0	65	66
SK	58.8	75.4	70	69.5	50.9	71.7	50	80	61.5	78.0	50	47
Esp	59.7	71.8	70	77.9	41.8	55.4	70	80	73.9	78.0	43	68
S	64.9	73.8	70	95.6	18.7	18.3	70	80	74.7	83.0	91	92
UK	77.8	81.1	85	90.8	50.6	50.7	90	90	73.9	88.0	90	86

Source: Heritage Foundation/Wall Street Journal (2012); www.heritage.org/index.
[a] This is the average of 7 (merged to 5) out of 10 indicators (monetary freedom, property rights and labour—data only for 2008—are excluded).

Table 5. Product market regulation and employment protection legislation

	Product Market Regulation[a]		Converted PMR[c]		Employment Protection[a,b]		Converted EPL[c]	
	1998	2008	1998	2008	1998	2008	1998	2008
Estonia	–	1.24	(79.3)	79.3	2.3[d]	2.1	61.7	65.0
Finland	2.01	1.12	66.5	81.3	2.1	2.0	65.0	66.7
France	2.45	1.39	59.2	76.8	3.0	3.1	50.0	48.3
Germany	2.00	1.27	66.7	78.8	2.3	2.1	61.7	65.0
Greece	2.91	2.30	51.5	61.7	3.5	2.7	41.7	55.0
Ireland	1.59	0.86	75.2	85.7	0.9	1.1	85.0	81.7
Italy	2.53	1.32	57.8	78.0	2.7	1.9	55.0	68.3
The Netherlands	1.59	0.91	73.5	84.8	2.7	2.0	55.0	66.7
Portugal	2.18	1.35	63.7	77.5	3.7	3.2	38.3	46.7
Slovakia	1.81[d]	1.54	69.8	74.3	1.8	1.4	63.3	70.0
Spain	2.47	0.96	58.8	84.0	2.9	3.0	51.7	50.0
Sweden	1.86	1.24	69.3	79.3	2.2	1.9	63.3	68.3
UK	1.01	0.79	83.2	86.8	0.6	0.8	90.0	86.7

Sources: Employment protection: OECD iLibrary (n.a.) and Tonin (2009, 479) (for Estonia 1998); Product market regulation: OECD Statistics Portal (n.a.).
[a] Scale 0 (no regulation/protection) − 4.5 (fully regulated/protected).
[b] version 1.
[c] 6 minus PMR score multiplied by 100/6.
[d] 2003.

In Table 5, we see the same trend of overall liberalisation as in Table 4. Liberalisation of PMR has, however, been stronger than liberalisation of EPL. In some countries, employment protection has even slightly risen (France, Ireland, Spain, UK). If one would make a comparative ranking, the one based on Table 5 would be similar to that of Table 4 with Britain and Ireland most liberal and the Mediterranean countries least so. Remarkable seems to be the big liberalisation jump Italy made here, while Finland and Ireland have made a big jump in the IEF statistics given in Table 4.

Now we can put together the IEF, PMR and EPL scores to calculate overall liberal values and, by subtracting them from 100, the overall embeddedness scores. Depending on the level of corruption, reality might differ, however, from the intentions of laws and other codified regulations on which the PMR and EPL indices are based. And corruption is part of embeddedness. So, it makes sense to adjust the PMR and EPL scores for corruption. I will do it by using the IEF corruption data. In Table 4, corruption determined the average scores by 20%. Giving corruption with respect to PMR and EPL the same weight as in Table 4, the formula to be applied in Table 6 is: ([2 × PMR] + [2 × EPL] + IEF-corruption)/5.

Like the previous two tables, this one shows that the differences between the countries are big. Overall, they have hardly narrowed: Britain and other north European countries are still considerably more liberal than southern countries, particularly Greece. Spain is the strongest liberaliser and the UK the least. This is not a value judgement, however. Without a strong liberal component, economies would not be capitalist, but to a higher or lower degree it coexists with statist, corporatist and patrimonial ingredients. Before looking at them, we can draw, based on Table 6, a figure (Figure 1) giving a glimpse of the location of our political economies on the axis between ideal-typical liberal capitalism and embedded capitalism.

Table 6. Overall liberal scores in 1998 and 2008

	Economic freedom average		Average of PMR and EPL adjusted for corruption		Overall liberal score		Extent of embeddedness	
	1998	2008	1998	2008	1998	2008	1998	2008
Estonia	74.4	78.9	70.4	71.1	72.4	75.0	27.6	25.0
Finland	60.4	79.2	70.8	78.4	65.6	78.8	34.4	21.2
France	58.5	66.9	57.7	64.8	58.1	65.9	41.9	34.1
Germany	67.0	71.8	68.0	73.5	67.5	72.7	32.5	27.3
Greece	55.3	58.3	47.3	55.5	51.3	56.9	48.7	43.1
Ireland	68.0	81.6	79.5	81.5	73.8	81.6	26.2	18.4
Italy	55.4	60.7	51.9	68.3	53.7	64.5	46.3	35.5
Netherlands	69.9	79.5	68.8	78.0	69.4	78.8	30.6	21.2
Portugal	61.7	64.3	53.8	62.9	57.8	63.6	42.2	36.4
Slovakia	58.8	75.4	63.2	67.1	61.0	71.3	39.0	28.7
Spain	59.7	71.8	52.8	67.2	56.3	69.5	43.7	30.5
Sweden	64.9	73.8	71.2	77.4	68.1	75.6	31.9	24.4
UK	77.8	81.1	87.9	86.6	82.9	83.9	17.1	16.1

1998

U_1 I_1 E_1 $N_1S_1D_1$ FI_1 Sk_1 $F_1P_1SP_1$ It_1 GR_1

2008

U_2 I_2 FI_2N_2 E_2S_2 D_2 Sk_2 SP_2 F_2It_2 P_2 GR_2

100   *75*   *50*   *25 0*

Liberal   **Embedded**

Figure 1. Location of selected European political economies on the axis between ideal-typical liberal and embedded capitalism in 1998 (T$_1$ grey) and 2008 (T$_2$ black). E = Estonia; FI = Finland; D = Germany; F = France; GR = Greece; IR = Ireland; IT = Italy; N = Netherlands; P = Portugal; Sk = Slovakia; SP = Spain; S = Sweden; U = United Kingdom

Indicating Levels and Change of Statism, Patrimonialism and Corporatism

For determining the levels of statism, patrimonialism and corporatism, the data required for at least some precision do not exist. For statism and patrimonialism, I will make use of the Worldwide Governance Indicators. The WGI data have a dichotomous structure positioning government effectiveness, regulatory quality and the rule of law on the one hand against control of corruption on the other hand. On the basis of these data, the space of embeddedness which was the residual value in Table 6 could be divided into statism and patrimonialism. An aspect of imprecision, however, is that corruption data from the IEF have already been an ingredient of the assessment of the levels of liberalism and embeddedness. Another one is that state effectiveness, regulatory quality and rule of law are not exactly the same as statism. And patrimonialism is more than only corruption. Moreover, for indicating the level of corporatism, only data for the mid-1990s are available for a number of the selected countries. Therefore, it is justifiable to label the levels of statism, patrimonialism and corporatism of our selected political economies as low, medium and high. This, despite its imperfect data basis, is still better than quantification only based on the rule of thumb.

Table 7 shows the scores of the WGI. They are scaled from -2.5 (worst performance) to 2.5 (best performance). In columns 7 and 8, the first three indicators are put together and converted into a scale from 0 to 100 providing the WGI score. This way the data are easier to read and to compare to those in preceding tables. A high WGI score will be interpreted as a high level of statism, although for this qualification the size of embeddedness has also to be taken into consideration. A high liberal/low embedded score plus a high WGI score therefore might result in a lower level of statism than results from a medium liberal score combined with less high WGI score. The scores on 'control of corruption' are kept separately because they are an indicator for the level of corruption: the lower the control of corruption, the higher is the corruption. For estimating this level, I will also look at the corruption scores in the IEF.

Remarkable in Table 7 is perhaps the high governance capacity of Ireland and the UK, the somewhat lower one of France and the decline of this capacity in 8 of the 13 countries during the period considered. That in 2008 the Italian capacity was lower than that of Greece is notable too. For the rest, the picture is familiar: the northern countries are doing better than the southern and eastern ones, but the gap is—leaving apart Italy and Greece—not as big as with previous indicators. Regarding corruption (the lower the score for control of corruption, the higher is the corruption), the situation is similar. Slightly ahead of Italy, Greece has the highest corruption score (for Greek details see Papadoulis 2006) and Finland the lowest, but equally worth mentioning is perhaps that Slovakia seems to combine a high and stable level of corruption with strong liberalisation (data from the Corruption Perception Index [Transparency International 2012] would not significantly change the picture).

What remains is the specification of corporatism. In the 1980s and 1990s, corporatism was a big issue in political economy. Attempts to comparatively measure its extent were also undertaken in those years. Siaroff (1999, 184f) has put together these attempts and produced an index of indices scaled $1-5$. Since there is no later one with a comparable scope, this is the index I will work with. Siaroff considers corporatism in Sweden and the Netherlands as high, in Finland and Germany as medium high, in Ireland as low to medium and in France, Italy and the UK as low. He also mentions Greece, Portugal and Spain, but because of the very limited number of quantitative investigations, he does not give them a score. From other research (Royo 2002) we know, however, that corporatism has a tradition on the Iberian peninsula and experienced some revival in the 1990s. Portuguese and Spanish corporatism should at least been ranked low to medium therefore. Greece, by contrast, does not have any corporatism worth mentioning (cf. Lavdas 2005), while analyses of corporatism in Estonia and Slovakia are missing.

In Table 8, the findings regarding statism, patrimonialism and corporatism are put together. Given the general rise of liberalism and the corresponding decrease of embeddedness since 1998 (Table 6, last two columns, and Figure 1), we can conclude that the levels of corporatism, statism and patrimonialism also decreased in most countries. In relation to each other, these levels increased or decreased in a few cases, however. Worth mentioning are Greece, Slovakia and perhaps Italy. In the table, this is indicated by arrows, though the weak and (in the case of corporatism) partially absent data urge cautiousness with specifications.

Table 7. Worldwide governance indicators 1998, 2008, scaled − 2.5 to 2.5

	1: Government effectiveness		2: Regulatory quality		3: Rule of law		Converted average of 1, 2 and 3[a]		4: Control of corruption (converted[a] after the slash)	
	1998	2008	1998	2008	1998	2008	1998	2008	1998	2008
Estonia	0.53	1.19	1.28	1.47	0.55	1.17	65.8	75.4	0.57/61.4	0.92/68.4
Finland	2.05	2.04	1.79	1.62	1.97	1.91	88.7	87.2	2.37/97.4	2.41/98.2
France	1.58	1.58	0.81	1.27	1.36	1.46	75.2	78.2	1.40/78.0	1.38/77.6
Germany	1.93	1.55	1.22	1.47	1.61	1.69	81.8	81.4	2.16/93.2	1.73/84.6
Greece	0.75	0.64	0.66	0.86	0.72	0.79	64.2	65.2	1.06/71.2	0.10/52.0
Ireland	1.78	1.53	1.69	1.92	1.59	1.75	84.4	84.6	1.58/81.6	1.76/85.2
Italy	0.87	0.37	0.74	0.91	0.76	0.34	65.8	60.8	0.52/60.4	0.18/53.6
Netherlands	2.07	1.61	1.89	1.77	2.17	1.74	90.8	84.2	2.27/95.4	2.16/93.2
Portugal	1.12	1.01	1.15	1.08	1.22	1.02	73.2	70.8	1.34/76.8	1.01/70.2
Slovakia	0.54	0.87	0.44	1.12	0.18	0.56	57.6	67.0	0.25/55.0	0.30/56.0
Spain	1.66	0.89	1.22	1.23	1.30	1.13	77.2	71.6	1.37/77.4	1.10/72.0
Sweden	1.99	1.91	1.19	1.67	2.22	1.77	86.0	85.6	2.23/94.6	2.23/94.6
UK	1.92	1.64	2.01	1.78	1.74	1.67	87.4	84.0	2.23/94.6	1.67/83.4

Source: World Bank (2011).
[a] − 2.5 is converted into 0, the original 0 into a converted 2.5, the original 2.5 into the converted 5 and all scores are multiplied by 20.

THE EUROPEAN UNION AFTER THE CRISIS

Table 8. *Relative* levels of statism, patrimonialism and corporatism in the space of embeddedness[a], 1990–2000

	Statism	Patrimonialism	Corporatism
Estonia	Low	Medium–high	–
Finland	Medium	Low	Medium–high
France	Medium–high	Medium	Low
Germany	Medium	Low–medium	Medium–high
Greece	Medium–high ↓	High ↑	Low
Ireland	Low–medium	Low–medium	Low–medium
Italy	Medium ↓ [b]	High ↑ [b]	Low
Netherlands	Medium	Low	High
Portugal	Medium–high	Medium	Low–medium
Slovakia	Low–medium ↑	High ↓	–
Spain	Medium	Medium	Low–medium
Sweden	Medium–high	Low	High
UK	Low–Medium	Low–medium	Low

Sources: Tables 4, 6 and 7 above; Siaroff (1999), Royo (2002) and Lavdas (2005).
[a] Arrows indicate change, no arrows indicate stability. The absence of arrows in Finland indicates that the relation of statism, patrimonialism and corporatism hardly changed, while the relative level of Greek patrimonialism increased at the cost of statism.
[b] Based on Table 6: ↓ = decline of 2.5–7.4 points; ↓ ↓ = 7.5–10 points; ↓ ↓ ↓ = >10 points.

How to Deal with Heterogeneity?

All countries live with some internal economic heterogeneity. In Italy and Belgium, it is strong, but both these countries also show how difficult it is to narrow the gap. Wallonia is still considerably poorer than Flanders, and the difference between northern and southern Italy is legendary. The differences between northern and southern Europe are similar. In the south, competitiveness is lower and corruption is higher. An additional special feature is the huge indebtedness of the southern countries, particularly of Greece. The debt problems have been created in the past by wrong decisions about membership in the Eurozone, by sleepy financial markets in the years up to 2008 and then by the burst of the bubble which compelled governments to bail out banks. A corruption-induced low state capacity to act enhanced the problems, and since 2009 austerity is worsening the social situation in the southern countries.

As indicated, Keynesian recipes raise serious questions and feed the illusion of a quick recovery. To narrow the gap will take time instead. Rich Ireland has left the problem zone, Spain has in any case left the ESFS programme (on 31 December 2013), Portugal just followed (18 May 2014) though caution seems still to be justified, Italy with its north–south divide remains a very special case, but for Greece the financial burden could overload its capacity. The EU therefore needs a scenario on certain conditions to bail out the Greek government. And it has to think about (bold) measures to bring down unemployment—particularly of juveniles in all southern member countries. In a transnational polity with strong national interests and complicated decision-making procedures, this is of course easier said than done—as is institutional reform with respect to patrimonialism (cf. Andrews 2013). Nonetheless, action is required. It should also involve a way to force the southern countries to raise their competitiveness. Alert financial markets and an alert ECB would not allow them cheap loans, but would lower interest rates when they attract FDI, modernise their economies and successfully fight corruption

29

and patronage. Positive incentives seem to be crucial. A break-up of the EU with internationally insignificant countries competing by devaluations and wage restraint is not a viable alternative.

Note

[1] In the IEF data (and PMR and EPL data in Table 5), the average country scores are relatively close to each other. Authoritarian countries (Belarus, Burma) are about half as liberal ('free') as the USA. This is due to the scaling of these indices. The IEF has hardly scores lower than 40 and in the PMR/EPL indices, the space above 3,5 (scale from 0 to 6) is completely empty. With scales eliminating much of the empty space, the differences between the countries would be larger.

References

Andrews, M. 2013. *The Limits of Institutional Reform in Development: Changing Rules for Realistic Solutions.* Cambridge: Cambridge University Press.

Becker, U. 2009. *Open Varieties of Capitalism. Continuity, Change and Performances.* Basingstoke: Palgrave Macmillan.

Becker, U. 2011. "Introduction." In *Change and Continuity in the Small West European Countries' Capitalisms,* edited by U. Becker, 11–44. Amsterdam: Amsterdam University Press.

Becker, U. 2013. "Measuring Change of Capitalist Varieties: Reflections on Method, Illustrations from the BRIC." *New Political Economy* 18 (4): 503–532.

Boyer, R. 2005. "How and Why Capitalisms Differ." *Economy and Society* 34 (4): 509–557.

Crouch, C. 2005. *Capitalist Diversity and Change. Recombinant Governance and Institutional Entrepreneurs.* Oxford: Oxford University Press.

De Grauwe, P. 2011. *The Governance of a Fragile Eurozone.* London: CEPS Working Document, no. 346.

European Commission. 2013. *Innovation Union Scoreboard 2013.* Brussels: European Commission.

Hall, P. A., and D. Soskice. 2001. "Introduction." In *Varieties of Capitalism. Institutional Foundations of Comparative Advantage,* edited by P. A. Hall and D. Soskice, 1–78. Oxford: Oxford University Press.

Heritage Foundation. 2012. *Index of Economic Freedom.* Washington: Heritage Foundation.

Intracen. 2012. *Trade Competitiveness Map.* Washington: International Trade Center. http://legacy.intracen.org/appli1/TradeCom/TP_TP_CI.aspx?RP=008&YR=2010

Jones, E. 2010. "Greek Competitiveness Is Not the Issue, Fiscal Discipline Is." *Eurointelligence.com,* 4 March.

Lavdas, K. A. 2005. "Interest Groups in Disjointed Corporatism: Social Dialogue in Greece and European 'Competitive Corporatism'." *West European Politics* 28 (2): 297–316.

OECD. 2009. *OECD in Figures 2009.* Paris: Organisation for Economic Co-operation and Development.

OECD. 2011. *Trade: Key Tables from OECD. Exports of Goods and Services as % of GDP.* Paris: Organisation for Economic Co-operation and Development.

OECD iLibrary. n.a. *Employment and Labour Market Statistics: Employment Protection Legislation.* Paris: Organisation for Economic Co-operation and Development. http://www.oecd-ilibrary.org/employment/data/employment-protection-legislation_lfs-epl-data-en

OECD Statistics Portal. n.a. *Indicators of Product Market Regulation (PMR). Integrate PRM Indicators.* Paris: Organisation for Economic Co-operation and Development. http://www.oecd.org/document/36/0,3746,en_2825_495698_35790244_1_1_1_1,00.html

Papadoulis, K. J. 2006. "Clientelism, Corruption and Patronage in Greece: A Public Administration Approach." *Teaching Public Administration* 26 (1): 13–24.

Polanyi, K. 1957. *The Great Transformation. The Political and Economic Origins of Our Time.* Boston: Beacon Press.

Price, V. 2013. *Greekonomics: The Eurocrisis and why Politicians Don't Get it.* London: Biteback.

Royo, S. 2002. "'A New Century of Corporatism?' Corporatism in Spain and Portugal." *West European Politics* 25 (2): 77–104.

Scharpf, F. 2013. "Entmündigung als Lösung? [From Paralysis to Solution?]." Friedrich Ebert Stiftung: *Internationale Politik und Gesellschaft.* [Online].

Schmidt, V. A. 2002. *The Futures of European Capitalism.* Oxford: Oxford University Press.

Siaroff, A. 1999. "Corporatism in 24 Industrial Democracies: Meaning and Measurement." *European Journal of Political Research* 36 (2): 175–205.

Tonin, M. 2009. "Employment Protection Legislation in Central and East European Countries." *South-East Europe Review* 4: 477–491.

Transparency International. 2012. *Corruption Perceptions Index 2008*. Berlin: Transparency International.

Weber, M. 1972. *Wirtschaft und Gesellschaft* [Economy and Society]. Tübingen: J.C.B. Mohr.

Wolf, A., J. Wagner, O. Röhn, and G. Nicoletti. 2010. *Product Market Regulation. Extending the Analysis Beyond OECD Countries*. OECD Economics Department, Working Paper 799. Paris: Organisation for Economic Coordination and Development.

World Bank. 2011. *Worldwide Governance Indicators*. Washington: World Bank. http://info.worldbank.org/governance/wgi/index.aspx#home

WTO. 2012. *Services Profiles*. Washington: World Trade Organization. http://stat.wto.org/ServiceProfile/WSDBServicePFReporter.aspx?Language=E

German Ordoliberalism as Agenda Setter for the Euro Crisis: Myth Trumps Reality

BRIGITTE YOUNG

University of Munster, Germany

ABSTRACT   *German political leaders have extolled the advantages of the rule-based ordoliberal doctrine as a panacea for the Eurozone countries to regain competitiveness. This legalistic doctrine has been used by the German Bundesbank as an important agenda setter to prevent alternative ideas from challenging the austerity discourse in the Eurozone. A closer look across German economic history tells a different story. At no time did perfect market competition work in practice as the ordoliberal doctrine postulates. In fact, it was the London Debt Agreement of 1953 with the Marshall Plan, and the combination of* Ordnungspolitik *with a more ethical and publicly provided social policy (what has become known as the* Soziale Marktwirtschaft) *which account for the German* Wirtschaftswunder. *But rather than rejecting* Ordnungspolitik *on the grounds that it is 'a dangerous idea', we should focus on institutional reforms based on an ethical and socially oriented economic model for the European Union (EU). In fact, this is what Germany has done since the 1950s, with the scales tipping sometimes in the direction of strengthening the ordoliberal side of competition policy, and at others shifting to more inclusive social measures. The question is whether Germany's 'real' economic history can provide a more realistic model for a sustainable social EU.*

1. Ideological Fragmentation in the Euro Zone

The present financial and economic crisis has split the Eurozone not only along geographical lines among northern current account surplus and southern deficit countries,[1] the fissure also reflects a deep ideological rift in how to resolve the financial and sovereign debt crisis in the Eurozone. Under the leadership of Germany, the current account surplus countries of Finland, Austria, and the Netherlands call for strict austerity rules to reign in fiscal deficits in the highly indebted Eurozone states (the so-called GIPSI countries of Greece, Ireland, Portugal, Spain, and Italy). The pressure for strict fiscal consolidation has only limited support among other European nations. In fact, many European government and political leaders have criticized Germany for its single-handed pursuit of austerity measures, its strict legal approach to the ECB mandate of monetary stability, and its export model which has contributed to the macroeconomic asymmetries in the Eurozone. Blyth (2013) has called austerity and the underlying ideational foundation of ordoliberalism as 'The History of a Dangerous Idea', since the policy of fiscal contraction has not promoted growth. Rather, the opposite has occurred. According to De Grauwe and Ji, the asymmetric fiscal adjustment between the debtor and creditor countries has produced a strong negative relation, i.e., 'the stronger the austerity programme, the deeper the decline in GDP' (2013, 3). This in turn is disputed by Wolfgang Schäuble, the German Finance Minister, who saw in the miniscule growth rate of some peripheral countries in Q3 2013 a silver lining. He declared in the *Financial Times* that 'Europe is being fixed' and one should 'ignore the doom-mongers' (Schäuble 2013, 9).

Keynesian economists have repeatedly warned of the pro-cyclical nature of the mandated austerity programs for indebted peripheral countries, since these policies leave no room for discretionary fiscal policy. Indebted countries are in a no-win situation: they confront unsustainably high budget deficits, but the austerity measures are more likely to harm aggregate demand and may aggravate the fiscal deficits of debtor nations even further (Heise 2012; De Grauwe and Ji 2013). In fact, the International Monetary Fund in reversing its policy stance pursued in the Asian crisis of 1997/1998 warned in the *World Economic Outlook 2012* that '(A)usterity alone cannot treat the economic malaise in the major advanced economies' (International Monetary Fund 2012, xvii). This has to do with the different impact of the multiplier in recessionary regimes. According to non-linear regime-dependent vector autoregression models, the fiscal multiplier varies with the state of the business cycle and the specific measures taken. Thus, in a recessionary regime, the multiplier is significantly stronger than in boom periods. The reason for this is that in a recession, the households are constrained by labor markets (spending of households depends on income and thus on employment, there are also credit and liquidity constraints on the product markets, and the financial intermediaries face constraints on the capital markets; see Mittnik and Semmler 2012). De Grauwe and Ji (2013) estimate that on average for every 1% increase in austerity, output declines by 1.4%. Not surprisingly, this multiplier measure of 1.4 produced a highly asymmetric trade-off in peripheral countries: a 1% improvement in government budget balances reduced GDP by 2.8% (De Grauwe and Ji 2013, 3).

Thus we confront a theoretical and empirical puzzle. Given that economic facts speak against fiscal consolidation in recessionary regimes, why do Germany and the other fiscal conservative countries insist on more austerity and fiscal consolidation in the hope of ensuring economic growth down the road? Explanations for this puzzle range from

(a) the German fear of a Weimar hyperinflation which, by the way, is wrongly associated with the rise of Hitler, but kept alive by the Bundesbank's rhetoric (Stern 2010),[2]
(b) the asymmetric power relations between creditor and debtor states which according to Dyson (2010) help explain different strategic interests and tactics in the crisis resolution,
(c) the strong endorsement of monetarism by the German Bundesbank (Abelshauser 2009).

In contrast to the above explanations, this article argues that the conservative German Bundesbank and many traditional economists adhere to a rule-based legalistic ordoliberal doctrine to prevent a more Keynesian alternative that would challenge the austerity discourse. Ordoliberalism, associated with the Freiburg School and the *Social Market Economy*,[3] calls for a political-economic order (Ordnungspolitik) which organizes competitiveness and competitive markets in such a way to prevent private power (in the form of industrial cartels and labor unions) and public power (socialist nationalization) from interfering with market forces. While ordoliberalism hails from the 1930s, some aspects of Ordnungspolitik were reintroduced into German debates after the sovereign debt crisis in the Eurozone, since German political leaders interpreted the sovereign debt crisis in peripheral countries as a lack of competitiveness of their economies.

In response to the crisis, the European Union (EU) was committed to save the Euro. The various measures (ranging from the Fiscal Pact, the Six-Pack, the European Semester) added up to creating a 'golden rule' (Grjebine 2012) through a legalistic rule-based system against the fiscal profligacy of member states. This 'ideological edifice behind German (ordoliberal) orthodoxy' (Dullien and Guérot 2012, 2) is strongly entrenched in German economic tradition and institutions such as the Federal Ministry of Finance, the Federal Ministry of Economics, the German Bundesbank, the Association for German Industry (BDI), and the Federal Association of the German Employers (BDA) (Abelshauser 2009). Not even the German political parties stray much from ideas of fiscal prudence and the importance of competition, as the recent Coalition Agreement between the Christian Democratic Union/Christian Social Union (CDU/CSU) and the Social Democratic Party (SPD) in November 2013 demonstrates. The Social Democrats fully endorsed the notion of price stability (perhaps in a more palatable form of *austerity light*) and competitive markets as the way out of the crisis. In fact, the Coalition Agreement mentions *competition* (Wettbewerb) and the *skill or ability to be competitive* (Wettbewerbsfähigkeit) 54 times in a 185 page document (Koalitionsvertrag 2013).

The paper is structured as follows. Section 2 introduces the ideas of ordoliberalism as deployed discursively by the German Bundesbank and some German mainstream economists. It is their belief that a return to a rule-based system of fiscal prudence is necessary to resolve the Eurozone crisis. At the centre of the analysis are the ordoliberal ideas of the *Freiburg School*. This approach is better able to explain why Germany's rule-based legal approach to the Euro crisis has led some academics to talk about the 'ordoliberalization of Europe' (Biebricher 2013, 6). Measures such as the strict adherence to fiscal discipline through a 'fiscal compact' which stipulates a constitutionally mandated 'debt brake' to limit the fiscal debt of all EU-countries, its defense of the independence of the Central European Bank, its strict adherence to price stability, and its support for recapitalizing banks through the European Stability Mechanism (ESM) (only on condition that the ESM would control banks which gain access to bail-out funds), reflect the ideas of *Ordnungspolitik* (Berghahn and Young 2013; Biebricher 2013; Dullien and Guérot 2012).

Section 3 provides a short overview of the ideological dispute among German economists which was played out in the printed media in the summer of 2012. Hans-Werner Sinn, the well-known director of the Munich-based ifo-Institute, co-signed a letter in the Frankfurter Allgemeine Zeitung (FAZ) on 5 July 2012 to warn against the European Banking Union, since the ordoliberal economists saw this as a ploy to introduce a mutualization of the Eurozone peripheral debt. The Keynesian reply was adamant in rejecting these charges. The dispute is important because it demonstrates the discursive agenda-setting power of ordoliberals to sway the German political terrain in their favor against the more Keynesian interventionist position within the German domestic arena. Section 4 goes back to ordoliberal ideas and points out the discrepancy between *myth and reality* in Germany's economic story telling. In fact, we have learned from historians that the doctrine of perfect competition and competitive markets and the anti-welfare rhetoric were never sufficient to account for Germany's economic miracle from the 1950s onward. Rather, the German model starting with the *Soziale Marktwirtschaft* under Ludwig Erhard in the 1950s was a combination of *Ordnungspolitik* and the 'social system of production' as practiced by the corporatist associations of the nineteenth century between employers and labor (Abelshauser 2009). Nor has Germany during the financial crisis of 2007/2008 and since the debt crisis followed ordoliberal ideas. In fact, the Coalition Agreement of 2013 is a sign that aspects of *Ordnungspolitik are* combined with social (Keynesian) measures. Given the historical German success story of the hybridization of ordoliberal and Keynesian ideas, it is cynical of Wolfgang Schäuble to advise the Eurozone peripheral countries to follow singularly the Freiburg doctrine to regain competitiveness.

2. German Ordoliberalism as Agenda Setter

The German Bundesbank with its mandate to guarantee price stability represents most strongly the rule-based ordoliberal doctrine within the German domestic arena. But these ideas are based on a broad consensus shared to a great extent across the political leadership and parties, the mainstream economic profession, the media, and the general public. Some members of the SPD and the Greens may sound more pro-European, but they equally endorse the austerity politics and the constitutionally mandated debt brake as evidenced by the SPD's endorsement of the Coalition Agreement of 2013. Ordoliberalism is not a new doctrine, since it has its antecedents in the 1930s. It was influential after WWII in the development of the Social Market Economy of Ludwig Erhard. Its most influential leaders are Walter Eucken, Franz Böhm, Wilhelm Röpke, Alfred Müller-Armack and Alexander Rüstow (Sally 1996; Bonefeld 2012; Berghahn and Young 2013; Young 2013). In the present Euro crisis resolution scenario, the influence of ordoliberalism is most evident in the German position on price stability and its defence of the independence of the Central Bank. The German Bundesbank was created and reflects the rule-based approach of an *economic order*, within which economic processes take place (Sally 1996, 235). After WWII, the ordoliberals argued for the primacy of currency policy. For Walter Eucken, monetary policy was the constituting principle of the *Ordnungspolitik:* 'All efforts to institute a competitive market economy will fail as long as price stability is not guaranteed' (cited in Issing 2000, 1). However, the goal of a sound monetary system was not just to guarantee price stability. Equally important were the rules for sanctions against any transgression of such price stability. The purpose was to rule out any discretionary space for central bankers to intervene in monetary policy (Young 2013).

German central bankers were eager to impose ordoliberal ideas into the governing modus of the European Central Bank. Once it became clear that the ECB violated the 'no-bail out clause' of the Maastricht Agreement in order to provide a bail-out for Greece in 2010, and later for Ireland, Portugal, and then also Spain, Axel Weber, German Chief economist at the ECB and some months later Jürgen Stark resigned in 2011. Nobody was particularly surprised when Jens Weidmann, the current president of the German Bundesbank, voted as the only member of the 23 member Board against the unlimited 'outright monetary transactions' (OMTs) program which the ECB Governing Council agreed on 6 September 2012 to start buying government bonds of indebted peripheral countries in the secondary markets. Before countries can qualify for this ECB program, they have to apply first to the ESM and accept strict fiscal conditionality. Mario Draghi's strongly worded support for the Euro 'to do whatever it takes' to protect the Eurozone from collapsing in July 2012 had the desired calming effect on the bond markets, so that the OMT program has not been used by any member state.

Since the German Bundesbank, but also Chancellor Angela Merkel and her finance minister Wolfgang Schäuble[4] see the fiscal profligacy of the indebted countries as the main culprit for declining competitiveness in the peripheral economies, the answer was seen in strengthening the Eurozone fiscal rules agreed under the Maastricht Treaty and the Stability and Growth Pact.[5] The new rules have automatic sanctions preventing governments from resorting to discretionary powers to violate the rules of *volonté générale*. Unlike in classical laissez-faire liberalism, the focus in ordoliberalism is not on private actors to ensure efficiency, but on the symbiosis of the state and the market to create the conditions for a competitive economy. Ordoliberalism rejects the neoclassical separation between the state and the market and argues that the 'invisible hand' of the price mechanism is insufficient to create the institutional framework for competitive markets. Thus, it is the state[6] which is called upon to create a constitutional framework, an *ordo*, within which market forces can operate freely. According to Walter Eucken, 'the economic constitution must be understood as a general political decision as to how the economic life of the nation is to be structured' (cited in Sally 1996, 234).

The dispute between German ordoliberal and Keynesian economists has much to do with the assumptions of how competitive markets function. The ECB transactions were seen by ordoliberal economists as violating the ECB's mandate and endangering its mandate of price stability. Since the Maastricht Treaty includes a no bail-out clause, ordoliberals saw in the ECB's action of OMTs a shift to common mutualization of debt in the form of Euro-bonds. Issing (2000), one of the architects of the Maastricht Agreement, warned that lax monetary policy and budget deficits lead to inflation and endanger political stability as happened during the Weimar period of the early 1920s.

3. Ordoliberalism Trumps Keynesianianism

A public letter drafted by the economic statistician Walter Krämer gained the necessary publicity and notoriety when the renowned Hans-Werner Sinn, director of the ifo-Institute Munich, was brought on board. The letter published in the business pages of the FAZ (2012), eventually signed by about 200 German economists, attacked the entire crisis resolution strategy of Angela Merkel as 'wrong' and warned, based on ordoliberal orthodoxy, that the proposed banking union would open the floodgates to socialize banking debts in the Euro zone and violate the mandate of the Maastricht Treaty. Tax payers, pensioners, and small depositors should be shielded from paying the foreseeable huge losses which would accrue from the inflationary spending orgy of southern countries. As if these dire warnings were not enough, they continued to berate politicians for their unavoidable inability to safeguard the mandated conditionality as long as the indebted countries have the majority vote in the ECB. Their parting shot was that neither the Euro nor the European idea will benefit from further rescue measures. It would only help Wall Street, the City of London and a string of indebted domestic and foreign banks.

It did not take long before German Keynesian economists countered with public rebuttals to save the economic profession from complete ridicule. Frank Heinemann, a Berlin economist, and Martin Hellwig, of the Max Planck Institute, Bonn, initiated with others a rebuttal declaring the banking union as essential since its proclaimed aim is to 'break the vicious circle between banks and sovereigns,' but only 'when an effective single supervisory mechanism is established.'[7] In the meantime, this second call also gathered more than one hundred supporters, ironically nine of which signed both the Krämer/Sinn call rejecting the Banking Union and the one supporting the political rescue measure. Another rebuke, entitled *Keine Schreckgespenster!* (No Bugbears), followed in the *Handelsblatt* (6 July 2012) drafted by Keynesians including Peter Bofinger, a member of the German Council of Economic Experts, Gustav Horn, director of the Institute of Macroeconomics, and others[8] criticizing the Krämer/Sinn text for fanning fear without providing substantive arguments. Not only do they deplore the damage Krämer/Sinn inflict on the political process, they deplore the damage done to the reputation of the German economic profession. In a public rebuttal, Gustav Horn attacked the nine economists who had signed both initiatives and called on them to at least distance themselves from the populist language of the Krämer/Sinn initiative.

This is not the end of the story. The German Council of Economic Advisors (also known as the five economic wise men) intervened in the dispute with a Special Advisory Opinion strongly supporting the EU summit decision to create a banking union, and suggesting further steps not precluding mutualization of Eurozone risks, a step Angela Merkel strictly rejects. Concretely, the Economic Advisors laid out details for a temporary euro area redemption fund, in which national debts above 60% are deposited, and guaranteed collectively by the Euro zone countries, retiring the debt over a period of 25 years (Sachverständigenrat 2012). Last but not least, the German pro-euro camp received support from the Institute for New Economic Thinking (INET) a New York think tank, funded in part by George Soros. The INET Council on the Euro Zone Crisis (ICEC), comprising 17 economists, including two of Germany's wise men, Peter Bofinger and Lars Feld, issued a *Master Plan* warning that Europe 'is sleep-walking into a catastrophe.' As an alternative to the present austerity course, they endorse both a banking union endowed with a banking license and a temporary redemption fund, arguing that the ESM is too small to help larger countries such as Spain and Italy (Süddeutsche Zeitung 2012).

Not surprisingly, the German government immediately rebuffed the Krämer/Sinn initiative claiming that they failed to cite the Euro-decision accurately, since the Euro Area Summit Statement of 29 June 2012 does not contain any reference to mutualising Euro zone debts (FAZ 2012). Equally sharp was the rebuke from Norbert Lammert, president of the German Bundestag, who in fact stated that of all the possible ways to provide input in resolving the Euro crisis, the least helpful was that of economists (Financial Times Deutschland 2012). But Hans-Werner Sinn did not stop simply with the Krämer/Sinn initiative. Addressing a hearing before the Federal Constitutional Court in Karlsruhe to decide the fate of the ESM in early July, he referred to the euro bailout as a 'bottomless pit,' as a 'machinery of asset destruction,' which did not offer a solution. In response to this bold attack, *Spiegel Online* ran an article asking 'Is the German Economist Exacerbating the Euro Crisis?' (Spiegel Online 2012).

While this clash of ideas can be shrugged off as a testosterone fuelled ego-trip among male academics, nevertheless it does demonstrate the agenda-setting power of ordoliberal ideas, and how difficult it is to go against the accepted myth of the historic role of ordoliberalism as the ideational foundation of the *Soziale Marktwirtschaft* and the 'Rhenish' model of capitalism. The problem for Keynesian economists is that austerity ideas play on familiar territory, since the rhetoric is anchored in a German tradition of frugality or 'living within your means,'[9] exemplified by Angela Merkel's reference to the 'Swabian Housewife'.

4. Myth and Reality About the German Economic Success Stories

Little work has been done to question the ordoliberal assumptions and whether these ideas were in fact as important for the German economic growth, first during the period of the 1950s and then as the ideational foundation for the Rhenish model as the present German leadership seems to imply. Is there any evidence

- that ordoliberal ideas alone had ushered in the *Wirtschaftswunder* of the 1950s?
- that ordoliberal ideas are the ideational foundation of the *Soziale Marktwirtschaft*, which in turn is used to explain the success of the Rhenish model of capitalism, or whether it is a myth due to a 'repressed history of origin'? (Abelshauser 2009)
- that Germany's turnaround from the 'sick man' of Europe in the 1990s to the present power engine of economic growth is the result of implementing ordoliberal ideas?
- that the much hailed 'ordoliberal success story' of Germany can be a model for southern Eurozone countries in order to become more competitive? (Schäuble 2012)

This section points to some discrepancies between the myth and the reality of ordoliberalism, while recognizing that much more nuanced work has to be done to demystify the ideological rhetoric and discourse of ordoliberalism and how it is instrumentalized by German political leaders and the German Bundesbank in extolling the virtues of ordoliberalism. Among German leaders, it has become fashionable to emphasize the advantages of the rule-based Social Market Economy as a panacea for the highly indebted countries in the Eurozone to regain their competitiveness. However, historians have repeatedly argued that there is a wide gulf between myth and reality, starting with the introduction of *the Soziale Marktwirtschaft*, a term coined by one of the ordoliberal thinkers, Alfred Müller-Armack, in 1947 (Abelshauser 2009; Berghahn 2010). In what follows, some neglected factors are highlighted in the present discourse on how Germany was able to overcome its indebtedness after WWII and start on its *Wirtschaftswunder* in the 1950s/1960s, and how it has continued to combine *Ordnungspolitik* with the *social* (albeit in a more restrictive form) to become the European locomotive after being declared the 'sick man' of Europe in the 1990s.

4.1 London Debt Agreement

The largely forgotten London Debt Agreement for Germany in 1953 helped to restore West Germany's debt sustainability and economic growth rates. Recent scholarship has shown that while the Marshall Plan was helpful in starting the German growth engine after WWII, it was the London Debt Agreement which was more important to get Germany back to economic growth (Kaiser 2013). The Tripartite Commission on the German Debt (the UK, France, and the USA), with representatives of 20 signatory states (including Greece, Ireland, Spain, Italy, and others), signed the agreement on 16 September 1953, relieving Germany of about 50% out of its total external debt (30 billion DM which included both pre- and post-war debts). The debt relief represented roughly 10% of West Germany's GDP in 1953, or 80% of its export earnings that year. This debt agreement was not only economically very generous, but in addition 'the implicit pardon was provided to a nation that had less than 10 years before inflicted upon the whole European continent and beyond the most devastating man-made catastrophe of modern history' (Kaiser 2013, 1). It surely is an irony of history that countries such Greece and other Eurozone indebted countries were signatories to this arrangement, and that Germany today is a creditor country but has learned little from its own history. It was not austerity and stringent structural reforms imposed on a war-torn Germany, but debt relief in combination with the Marshall Plan, that helped Germany regain access to international capital markets and ensure its economic strength. For the remaining debt repayment, interest arrears were reduced by one-quarter and were locked in between 4% and 5%. This meant that annual payments in terms of external debt service were set at fairly low levels, representing never more than 5% of Germany's annual export earnings. In concluding, Kaiser points to four factors that made the London Debt Agreement successful and could serve as a model for the indebted Eurozone countries today:

1. The conference set up negotiations between debtor and creditor countries among equals, rather than imposing the wishes of the war winners and creditors.
2. The London Debt Agreement differed in that it considered the totality of external debt obligations in order to permit a fresh start for the entire West German economy.
3. The debt sustainability was based on the ability of Germany to cover the debts out of its current trade surplus in order to avoid drawing on Germany's monetary reserves.
4. And finally, the London Debt Agreement established six arbitrational dispute mechanisms to resolve disputes through consultation.

It surely is one of the most ironic aspects that Herman-Josef Abs, the head of the German delegation to the London Debt Agreement, rejected any call for austerity and structural reforms. Abs 'considered the specific provision that Germany should pay its debt service exclusively out of current trade surpluses and not by taking recourse to reserves or new debt, as an *explicit rejection of Anglo-Saxon austerity*" (emphasis by B.Y.).' German trade surpluses were also facilitated by its creditors and trading partners by tacitly tolerating the gross undervaluation of its currency (Kaiser 2013, 18).

4.2 The Myth That Perfect Market Competition Was the 'Best Social Policy'

Despite the present German rhetoric that peripheral countries have to regain their competitiveness through fiscal consolidation, structural adjustments, and cuts in welfare spending, the German praxis during the introduction of the *Soziale Marktwirtschaft* by Chancellor Erhard tells a different story. As the well-known German historian Abelshauser notes, ordoliberals of that period argued for a *liberal interventionism* against a regulative Keynesian interventionism. Liberal interventionism implied that real markets should come close to perfect competitive markets (vollkommener Wettbewerbsmarkt). The state through an independent Cartel office and a Central Bank are to monitor and control the development of such a competitive order. Competitiveness was based on a price policy which makes it possible to create market conditions 'as if a perfect competitive market exists in actuality' (Abelshauser 2009, 13–14, citing Franz Böhm). The role of the *social* in ordoliberal thinking has led to confusing interpretations. It seems that ordoliberals regarded social policy as an inherent aspect of *Ordnungspolitik*, implying that a well-functioning competitive market would not need a social policy (Sally 1996). In particular, Chancellor Erhard regarded an expansive economic policy as the best social policy. Despite Erhard's famous title of his book 'Wohlstand für Alle' (Prosperity for all), social did not mean a correction of market failures.

It soon became apparent that the aspiration and reality between price development on the one hand, and profits and wages on the other widened. This was particularly evident in the increasing poverty rate among retirees whose pension payments had stayed low. They could no longer rely on private savings, since they were mostly destroyed through two wars, inflation, and forced displacement from the Eastern territories. The swelling discontent of the retirees was only halted once Chancellor Konrad Adenauer introduced the pension reforms in 1957. These measures stipulated a pay-as-you-go system (*Umlageverfahren*), increases in the annuity rate, and a dynamic adjustment of the level of pensions to gross domestic product. As a result, the ordoliberals had to give up their ambition to achieve social policy via perfectly competitive markets starting at the end of the 1950s. Under the Grand Coalition (between CDU/CSU and SPD) in the 1960s, the Economic Minister Karl Schiller was able to provide the synthesis between the Freiburg doctrine and the Keynesian message. This was then institutionalized through *the Konzertierte Aktion* between labor unions and business associations and became commonly known as *Modell Deutschland* (Abelshauser 2009).

Surely, many may object to this kind of storytelling and argue that Germany has long crossed the Rubicon since the social democratic government reforms of Gerhard Schröder, and as a result Germany is as neoliberal as the Anglo-Saxon countries today (Bruff and Ebenau 2012). Undoubtedly, there is some truth to this argument. However, even during the time of the social policy reforms of Agenda 2010 and the introduction of the Hartz labor market reforms by the SPD, the government did not impose all the hardship on German citizens. Instead, the German government chose to violate the Maastricht Treaty of the mandated 3% fiscal deficits from 2003 to 2005. This permitted the German government more flexibility in its fiscal policies, an adjustment which the German government denies to the sovereign debt countries today. Similarly, Angela Merkel does not tire of invoking discursively the need for more competition in the EU member states and thus continues to emphasize the importance of *Ordnungspolitik*. At the same time, the Coalition Agreement has many social aspects, such as the increased pension for mothers who had children before 1992, the retirement at 63 years for workers who have paid into the pension fund for 45 years, and a floor for the minimum wage of €8.50 for low-skilled workers.

A brushstroke across German economic history shows that the scales tipped in the direction of strengthening the ordoliberal side of competition policy at some points in time, and at others shifted to more extensive social measures. The important point is, however, that perfect market competition was deployed at a discursive level, but not necessarily adhered to in practice as the ordoliberals had postulated.

The question is whether Germany's 'real' history of its economic success story can provide a more realistic model for the EU.

5. Conclusion: The 'Real' Soziale Marktwirtschaft as a Possible Model for the EU?

This article agrees with the critics that Germany's insistence on more austerity and price deflation, using ordoliberal ideas as the justification for such deflationary policies, will not make peripheral countries more competitive. It is also true, as Scharpf (2013) argues, that any solutions to the three crises facing the Eurozone (sovereign debt crisis; deflationary demand, and current account deficits in the peripheral countries) will contradict each other and make the crisis even worse. Namely, if in accordance with Keynesian policies demand in the indebted countries in increased and this is done via higher imports, then the current account deficit will rise, nominal wages would increase again, and this would decrease any gains in competitiveness (Scharpf 2013, 5).

But rather than polarizing the academic discussion between those arguing that ordoliberalism is a dangerous idea (Blyth 2013), that the 'political philosophy of ordoliberalism amounts to a view of politics that is authoritarian, undemocratic and technocratic' (Biebricher 2013) to altogether denying that EU reforms are in the ordoliberal tradition (Jabko 2013), I suggest that we should demystify ordoliberalism and realize that from the start of the *Soziale Marktwirtschaft* ordoliberal ideas and its emphasis on competitive markets and fiscal frugality cannot account for the successful German economic model. Historians have shown that the implementation of competitive markets and an anti-welfare doctrine led to social hardship during the Erhard regime. As a result, and despite opposition from the ordoliberals, the *Ordnungspolitik* was subsequently combined with a more ethical doctrine of social Catholicism espoused already in the Quadragesimo Anno, 1931 (cited in Hien 2013) and institutionalized during the corporatist *Konzertierte Aktion* between labor unions and employer associations in the 1960s. Thus, we should neither reject ordoliberal ideas to create an institutional framework for the Eurozone out of hand, nor elevate it to an ideational 'one-size-fits-all' economic model to be adopted for the diverse European member states. We should focus on an institutional rule-based framework and combine it with an ethical and socially oriented model to build a EU which inspires once again the loyalty and trust of its citizens. In fact, this is nothing less than the present Pope Francis has called for in his 'Evangelii Gaudium', advocating a shift to a more ethical, inclusive, and social capitalism (Huffington Post 2013).

Acknowledgments

The author thanks the two reviewers for their constructive comments, as well as Hans-Jürgen Bieling for his input on the importance of the German Rentenreform 1957, and Ian Bruff for his critique of ordoliberalism. A special appreciation goes to Hugo Radice for his comments and for organizing the journal issue. As a disclaimer, the final responsibility rests with the author.

Notes

[1] The current account surplus countries include Germany, Austria, Holland, Finland, and Luxemburg, while deficit countries include Ireland, Spain, Greece, Cyprus, Portugal, and Italy.

[2] In fact, it was the high unemployment rate due to the restrictive fiscal policies of the Reichs-Chancellor, Heinrich Brüning (1930–1932), a course which was also tolerated by the Social Democrats, which paved the way for the rise of National-Socialism and Hitler's political ascendancy.

[3] There is some new debate about whether ordoliberal ideas are the ideational foundation of the Social Market Economy of the 1950s introduced under Chancellor Ludwig Erhard (see Abelshauser 2009; Berghahn 2010).

[4] Wolfgang Schäuble not only mentions in his speeches that he was born in Freiburg, he seems to infer from this coincidence that he is a 'natural' ordoliberal adherent (Schäuble 2012).

[5] Many critics point out that Germany first, and then France, violated the Maastricht Agreement between 2003 and 2005. It is for this reason that Angela Merkel insists that the rules have to be strictly set and implemented with automatic sanctions so that larger countries, such as Germany and France, can no longer violate the rules.

⁶ There is a debate on whether the original ordoliberal thinkers continued to adhere to their 'strong State thesis' after the war (as initially advocated in the 1930s) after their experience with the Nazi dictatorship. The strong state was thought to be a prerequisite to intervene against the formation of private and public monopolies and oligopolies (Bonefeld 2012). After 1945, the role of the *strong* state was much less emphasized during the *Soziale Marktwirtschaft*. This has to do with their first-hand experience with Nazi Germany and their subsequent shift to a more constitutional framework sanctioned by legitimate parliaments (Berghahn and Young 2013). In many respects, the 'strong state argument' is no longer of theoretical importance, since the present ordoliberal scholars have shifted to a more constitutional economic approach, starting with Viktor Vanberg (see Vanberg 1988; Feld and Köhler 2011).

⁷ Euro Area Summit Statement, Brussels, 29 June 2012.

⁸ Others include Michael Hüther, Dalia Marin, Bert Rürop, Friedrich Schneider, and Thomas Straubhaar (see Handelsblatt 2012, 8).

⁹ Also the German language seems to normatively intervene in putting the surplus and debtor countries along a good and bad axis. Surplus countries are in the good camp, whereas the debtor countries are not only 'bad', they are also *schuldig* (meaning guilty) in their state of affairs. A debtor is thus a Schuldner (somebody who is personally implicated in the debt and by implication has to atone and/or suffer for the sins committed).

References

Abelshauser, Werner. 2009. *Des Kaisers neue Kleider? Wandlungen der Sozialen Marktwirtschaft* [The Kaiser's New Clothes? Changes in the Social Market Economy], 1–41. Munich: Roman Herzog Institut.

Berghahn, Volker. 2010. *Ludwig Erhard, die Freiburger Schule, und das Amerikanische Jahrhundert* [Ludwig Erhard, the Freiburg School, and the American Century]. Freiburger Diskussionspapiere zur Ordnungsökonomik, 10/1 [Freiburg Discussion Paper on Ordnungs-Economic, 10/1], 1–12. Freiburg: Walter Eucken Institut.

Berghahn, Volker, and Brigitte Young. 2013. "Reflections on Werner Bonefeld's 'Freedom and the Strong State: On German Ordoliberalism' and the Continuing Importance of the Ideas of Ordoliberalism to Understand Germany's (Contested) Role in Resolving the Euro Zone Crisis." *New Political Economy* 18 (5): 768–778.

Biebricher, Thomas. 2013. "Europe and the Political Philosophy of Neoliberalism." *Contemporary Political Theory* 12 (4): 338–350.

Blyth, Mark. 2013. *Austerity. The History of a Dangerous Idea*. Oxford: Oxford University Press.

Bonefeld, Werner. 2012. "Freedom and the Strong State: On German Ordoliberalism." *New Political Economy* 17 (5): 633–656.

Bruff, Ian, and Matthias Ebenau. 2012. "Verabschiedet euch vom 'Modell Deutschland!' [Say Good-Bye to the 'German Model!']." Cicero Online. April 5. http://www.cicero.de//weltbuehne/britische-kritik-am eu-krisenkurs-verabschiedet-euch-vom-modell-deutschland/48871

De Grauwe, Paul, and Yuemei Ji. 2013. "The Legacy of Austerity in the Eurozone." Centre for European Policy Studies. Downloaded December 20. http://www.ceps.eu

Dullien, Sebastian, and Ulrike Guérot. 2012. *The Long Shadow of Ordoliberalism: Germany's Approach to the Euro Crisis*. Policy Brief. London: European Council on Foreign Relations.

Dyson, Kenneth. 2010. "Norman's Lament: The Greek and Euro Area Crisis in Historical Perspective." *New Political Economy* 15 (4): 597–608.

Feld, Lars P., and Ekkehard A. Köhler. 2011. "Ist die Ordnungsökonomik zukunftsfähig? [Does Ordnungs-Economics have a Future?]" *Zeitschrift für Wirtschafts- und Unternehmensethik (zfwu)* 12 (2): 173–195.

2012. "Ökonomieschelte." *Financial Times Deutschland*, July 9, p. 14.

FAZ (Frankfurter Allgemeine Zeitung). 2012. "Protestaufruf. Hans-Werner Sinn und Walter Krämer. Der offene Brief der Ökonomen im Wortlaut [Proclamation. Hans-Werner Sinn und Walter Krämer. An Open Letter of Economists]." *Wirtschaft*, July 5.

Grjebine, André. 2012. "The Radical Reform That Should Be on the Agenda in Brussels." *FT*, October 18, p. 9.

Handelsblatt. 2012. "Keine Schreckgespenster! [No Scare Specters!]." Peter Bofinger, Gustav Horn, Michael Hüther, Dalia Marin, Bert Rürup, Friedrich Schneider und Thomas Straubhaar, 6.7: 8.

Heise, Arne. 2012. "Governance Without Government or: The Euro Crisis and What Went Wrong with European Economic Governance." Discussion Paper. ISSN 1868-4947/32. Zentrum für Ökonomische und Soziologische Studien, Universität Hamburg.

Hien, Josef. 2013. "The Ordoliberalism That Never Was." *Contemporary Political Theory* 12 (4): 349–358.

Huffington Post. 2013. "Pope Francis 'Evangelii Gaudium' Calls for Renewal of Roman Catholic Church, Attacks 'Idolatry of Money'." November 26.

International Monetary Fund. 2012. *World Economic Outlook.* Washington, DC: International Monetary Fund.

Issing, Otmar. 2000. "Walter Eucken: Vom Primat der Währungsunion [Walter Eucken: About the Primacy of the Currency Union]." Vortrag: Freiburg Walter Eucken Institut [Lecture: Freiburg Walter Eucken Institute]. March 17. http://www.ecb.int

Jabko, Nicolas. 2013. "Re-problematizing Neoliberalism." *Contemporary Political Theory* 12 (4): 360–366.

Kaiser, Jürgen. 2013. *One Made It Out of the Debt Trap. Lessons from the London Debt Agreement of 1953 for Current Debt Crisis,* 1–24. Berlin: Friedrich-Ebert-Stiftung, Department for Global Policy Development. ISBN 978-3-86498-584-3. http://www.fes-globalization.org

2013. "Koalitionsvertrag CDU/CSU, SPD, Deutschlands Zukunft Gestalten [Coalition Agreement CDU/CSU, SPD, Shaping Germany's Future]." November 27. http://www.tagesschau.de/inland/koalitionsvertrag136.pdf

Mittnik, Stefan, and Willi Semmler. 2012. "Regime Dependence of the Multiplier." *Journal of Economic Behavior and Organization* 83 (3): 502–522.

Sachverständigenrat zur Begutachtung der gesamtwirtschaftlichen Entwicklung [Expert Council to Evaluate the Overall Economic Development]. 2012. "Nach dem EU-Gipfel [After the EU-Summit].". Special Expert Opinion. July 5. http://www.sachverstaendigenrat-wirtschaft.de/fileadmin/dateiablage/download/publikationen/sg2012.pdf

Sally, Razeen. 1996. "Ordoliberalism and the Social Market: Classical Political Economy from Germany." *New Political Economy* 1 (2): 233–257.

Scharpf, Fritz W. 2013. "Entmündigung als Lösung? Noch mehr Souveränitätsverzicht kann den Euro auch nicht retten [Disenfranchisement as Solution? Additional Renunciation of Sovereignty cannot save the Euro either]." *Internationale Politik und Gesellschaft (IPG)* 1–6. http://www.ipg-journal.de/schwerpunkt-des-monats/die-zukunft-der-europaeischen-union/artikel/detail/entmuendigung-als-loesung/

Schäuble, Wolfgang. 2012. "Auf dem Weg aus der Krise—Was haben wir gelernt? Was muss sich ändern? [On the Way out of the Crisis—What have we Learned? What needs to Change?]." Abschluss-Vortrag von Bundesfinanzminister Dr. Wolfgang Schäuble im Saal der 17. Handelsblatt Jahrestagung in Frankfurt/Main [Concluding Presentation by the Federal Finance Minister Dr. Wolfgang Schäuble at the Handelsblatt Annual Meeting in Frankfurt/Main], September 5. Bundesministerium der Finanzen. http://www.bundesfinanzministerium.de/Content/DE/Reden/2012/2012-09-05-Handelsblatt-Jahrestagung.html

Schäuble, Wolfgang. 2013. "Ignore the Doom-mongers—Europe Is Being Fixed." *Financial Times,* September 17.

Spiegel Online. 2012. "Professor Propaganda. Is German Economist Exacerbating Euro Crisis?." July 7. http://www.spiegel.de/international/business/hans-werner-sinn-s-simplistic-euro-crisis-theories-divide-german-economists-a-844590.html

Stern, Fritz. 2010. *Fünf Deutschland und ein Leben* [Five Germany and one Life]. München: Deutscher Taschenbuch Verlag.

Süddeutsche.de. 2012. "Schlafwandelnd in die Katastrophe." July 25. http://article.wn.com/view/2012/07/25/Schuldenkrise_Schlafwandelnd_in_die_Katastrophe/

Vanberg, Viktor. 1988. "'Ordnungstheorie' as Constitutional Economics. The German Conception of a 'Social Market Economy'." ORDO—*Jahrbuch für die Ordnung von Wirtschaft und Gesellschaft* 39: 17–31.

Young, Brigitte. 2013. "Ordoliberalismus—Neoliberalismus—Laissez-faire-Liberalismus [Ordoliberalism—Neoliberalism—Laissez-faire-Liberalism]." In *Theorien der Internationalen Politischen Ökonomie* [Theories of International Political Economy], edited by Joscha Wullweber, Antonia Graf, and Maria Behrens, 33–48. Wiesbaden: Springer VS.

Exploring the Keynesian–Ordoliberal Divide. Flexibility and Convergence in French and German Leaders' Economic Ideas During the Euro-Crisis

FEMKE A.W.J. VAN ESCH
Utrecht University, The Netherlands

ABSTRACT   *The Euro-crisis is the most severe crisis the European Union has ever faced. Despite its scale and urgency, political and financial leaders have struggled to find its solution. Several observers have traced this inability back to the divide between states adhering to Ordoliberal and those advocating Keynesian policies, Germany and France in particular. Preceding the question of whether and how leaders' policy ideas influenced decision-making, however, is the question to what extent such paradigmatic divide actually existed. To provide an in-depth and dynamic view of the French and German divide, this study uses the technique of Comparative Cognitive Mapping to explore the extent to which the views of Chancellor Merkel, President Sarkozy and the German and French central bank presidents, Weber and Noyer, may be characterised as Ordoliberal or Keynesian. Moreover, the article analyses how the crisis affected these ideas. The study finds that in paradigmatic terms, leaders' policy views are rather ambiguous and flexible. Moreover, it shows that the Euro-crisis actually fostered a convergence in views towards a more modest Ordoliberal view rather than a greater divide. Remarkably, this convergence moves the group consensus towards a more compromising position, away from the traditional position of the dominant partner, Germany.*

1. Introduction

The current Euro-crisis is the most severe crisis the European Union (EU) has faced since its inception. Despite its overwhelming scale and urgency, EU political and financial leaders have struggled to find an answer to the problems. Several observers have traced this inability back to the divide between states adhering to Ordoliberal and those advocating Keynesian policies, Germany and France in particular (Van Esch 2012; Blyth 2013; Hall 2012; Krotz and Schild 2012; Segers and Van Esch 2007). As the criticism of Merkel's reticent Ordoliberal response and the clashes between German central bankers and their peers at the European Central Bank (ECB) suggest, the divide seemed especially detrimental at the level of French and German political and financial leaders. In their position of top national representatives in the European Council and the ECB, they played a key and highly contested role in the decision-making surrounding the Euro-crisis.

Their lack of common understanding on the causes and nature of the crisis is seen as hampering crisis decision-making and exacerbated the self-fulfilling prophecy dynamics already inherent to crisis by further diminishing market-trust. Preceding the question of whether and in what way leaders' policy ideas influenced crisis-decision making, however, is the question to what extent such paradigmatic divide actually existed and how sustainable it was in light of the outbreak of the crisis. Claims of actors' adherence to Keynesian or Ordoliberal ideas are often based on a black and white, unitary and rigid conceptualisation of policy paradigms that deny the complexity, ambiguity and malleability of political views found in real life. Ambiguity and flexibility provide opportunities for political bargaining, social learning, persuasion and compromise, the very fabric politics is made of (Carstensen 2011; Wincott 2004).

In order to provide a more detailed and dynamic view of the French and German divide, this study provides an in-depth analysis of the extent to which leaders adhered to the ideal type Keynesian–Ordoliberal paradigm. To do so, the article introduces and extents the technique of Comparative Cognitive Mapping (CCM). This technique, which has firm roots in political and social psychology, is one of the few methods available that allows for the systematic, in-depth analysis of leaders' policy ideas (Van Esch 2012; Axelrod 1976; Young and Schafer 1998). It will be used to explore to which extent the policy ideas of the German chancellor Merkel, Bundesbank president Weber, French President Sarkozy and governor of the Banque de France, Noyer, may be characterised as Ordoliberal or Keynesian. Moreover, the article will study how the Euro-crisis affected these ideas and whether this resulted in an exacerbation or reduction of the differences in view. In doing so, it sheds light on one of the key empirical puzzles in European Studies of this time and addresses a key unresolved question in European Studies and crisis-management studies: To what extent do crises foster ideational change or rigidity and induce policy-consensus (Deverell 2009; Schmidt 2010)?

2. Ordoliberal–Keynesian Divide

In European studies, structural and institutional theory has long provided the dominant perspective. However, more and more scholars acknowledge that policy-ideas of pivotal political decision-makers influence politics and decision-making (Blyth 1997; Carstensen 2011; Hall 1993; Parsons 2002; Schmidt 2008, 2010). European economic and monetary integration is one of the domains in which scholars have long argued that ideational factors play a significant role (Dyson and Featherstone 1999; Kaelberer 2002; Marcussen 1999; McNamara 1998; Verdun 1999). Especially, the division between Ordoliberalism and Keynesianism is perceived as highly relevant to understand the incomplete or 'irrational' design of European Economic and Monetary Union (EMU) and the Stability and Growth Pact (SGP) and ineffective Euro-crisis leadership (Van Esch 2012, 2013;Blyth 2013; Dullien and Guerot 2012; Hall 2012; Howarth and Rommerskirchen 2013; Segers and Van Esch 2007).

When taken as an ideal type, the Ordoliberal view is characterised first and foremost by a belief in the primacy of price stability ('sound money'), which is the guiding principle by which all other policy-measures are assessed. Crucially, in the eyes of the Ordoliberals, there is no trade-off between price stability on the one hand, and employment and economic growth on the other. To ensure price stability, European economic and monetary integration must meet two requirements. First, it has to ensure that member states adopt stringent budgetary and fiscal policies and denounce monetary financing. Second, Ordoliberals stress the need for CB independence, as only a Central Bank that is constitutionally, politically and financially autonomous will guarantee sound and credible monetary policy-making based on expert analysis of the economic fundamentals, rather than on political or electoral considerations. Finally, Ordoliberals combine these economic ideas with ardent support for the primacy of economic over political or geo-political considerations.

In the Keynesian perspective, price stability is not regarded as the most salient economic goal nor is price stability perceived to be the ultimate goal of economic policy. Second, in their eyes, a trade-off does exist between economic growth and employment on the one hand, and price stability on the other. In addition, economic stimulation—achieved for instance through government spending—as opposed to stringent budgetary policy is promoted to foster economic growth and employment. These economic benefits are seen to outweigh possible effects on budgetary discipline and price stability. In terms of the mandate of the ECB, Keynesians may thus advocate extending its central tasks to include other goals than the mere guarding of price stability. Since within the institutional configuration of EMU, goals such as fiscal and financial stability are assigned to political actors, Keynesians generally show less devotion to ECB independence than Ordoliberals (Van Esch 2012; Dullien and Guerot 2012).

If regarded as ideal types, these economic paradigms clearly advocate very different, even contradictory views on what constitutes 'sound' economic policy and it is readily imaginable that hawkish adherence to them may inhibit unified European policy-making (cf. Hall 1993). However, such black and white and rigid conceptualisation of policy paradigms denies the complexity, ambiguity and malleability of political views found in real life and it is unclear to what extent key policy-makers actually subscribed to these paradigms or persisted in their views when faced with the Euro-crisis and conflicting views of significant peers.

3. Policy Ideas, Change and Convergence

In recent years, scholars in various branches of political and policy-science have studied the role of ideas in politics and policy-making. Ideas are subjective beliefs on how the world works and what is perceived as good or bad (Levy 1994; Schmidt 2008). Such ideas need not be 'true' or rational in the sense of being obtained through a thorough weighing costs and benefits. Actors are, however, assumed to reason with some consistency and to be 'rational' within the boundaries of their own subjective views.

Moreover, despite the multitude of different concepts used in different traditions, most authors make a distinction between ideas on two or three levels of abstraction (Van Esch 2007; Goldstein and Keohane 1993; Hall 1993; Levy 1994; Sabatier and Jenkins-Smith 1993; Schmidt 2008): (1) *diagnostic ideas* concerning the nature of things, state of affairs and circumstances at hand; (2) *instrumental ideas* concerning the causal relations and mechanisms that connect events and instruments to ultimate goals and values and (3) *principled ideas* that encompass the goals actors strive for, be they normative or utilitarian in nature. Combined, the related set of these different ideas form an actor's worldview. This worldview may be more or less in accordance with a policy paradigm (Wincott 2004).

As for the flexibility of these ideas, some scholars argue that they are especially volatile in times of crisis when dominant views are challenged and windows-of-opportunity arise for alternative views to gain weight. Moreover, crises intensify interaction between small groups of decision-makers which facilitates persuasion, emulation and learning (Van Esch 2007; Deverell 2009). However, advocates of the rivalling *threat-rigidity thesis* argue that crises limit decision-making time, narrow leaders' perceptual field and diminish their information-processing capacity (Staw, Sandelands, and Dutton 1981; Steinbruner 1974). They thereby inhibit learning and induce leaders to fall back on, and fortify their pre-existing views. Previous studies into this debate suggest that both patterns occur empirically (Boin, 't Hart, and Van Esch 2012; Stern and Sundelius 1997).

In addition, most scholars argue that some ideas are more pivotal than others. This is especially relevant because such pivotal ideas are deemed more stable than peripheral ideas, and when policy learning occurs 'it is usually confined to the secondary aspects of belief systems' (Sabatier and Jenkins-Smith 1993; Renshon 2008; Steinbruner 1974). However, once a change in core or dominant beliefs occurs, this is expected to have a cascading effect, resulting in a grand-scale revision of an actor's views. In this line of thinking, paradigm shifts are seen as some sort of U-turn in the sense of a complete replacement of an Ordoliberal worldview for Keynesian ideas. Such dialectic conceptualisation of paradigms and ideational change denies the complexity, ambiguity and malleability of political views and underestimates the opportunity for political bargaining, social learning, persuasion and compromise, the very fabric politics is made of (Carstensen 2011; Wincott 2004). Moreover, it overlooks the empirical finding that actors may not only exhibit rigidity or a reversal of views, their ideas may simply be reduced or reinforced in strength. To allow for a more nuance view, this study will explicitly distinguish between *reversal, reduction, reinforcement* and *stability* of views and operationalise change as a spectrum rather than either/or category (Van Esch 2007; Renshon 2008). A reversal of ideas refers to a paradigmatic U-turn like a shift from an Ordoliberal to a Keynesian worldview. The reduction and reinforcement of ideas, respectively, involve the mere weakening or strengthening of the paradigmatic orthodoxy of ideas.

When one accepts that ideas are subjective and similar circumstances steer actor's views in different directions, it is clear that ideational change does not necessarily foster a convergence towards a shared perspective. The propensity for convergence depends on the mechanism that leads to change. 'Social' forms of learning such as emulation, persuasion and socialisation are more likely to induce a meeting of minds than individual forms of learning (Burnell and Reeve 1984; Checkel 2001). Different contexts may be more or less conducive for social learning. In European studies, for instance, some argue that central bankers form an 'epistemic community' due to the frequency with which they meet, their relative isolation from daily political scrutiny and the high level of expertise (Beyers 2005; Checkel 2001; Verdun 1999). Moreover, more than the political leaders whose major constituencies have distinct national interests and cultural dispositions, central bankers are speaking to the globalised financial markets and its observers. This would lead us to believe that ideational convergence is more likely among central bankers than political leaders. In addition, French and German leaders clearly faced different pressures for ideational change during the crisis. Despite its growing debt, Germany was seen as Europe's economic giant and remained relatively unaffected by the crisis: it maintained its Triple A status and briefly even enjoyed negative sovereign bond yields. While Merkel was criticised for her reticent crisis management style and suffered a decline in public approval rates, overall there were few incentives to deviate from her original policy-position. France was hit harder by the crisis. Despite the loss of its Triple A status and continuous criticism of its economic policies in the Anglo-American press, however, its sovereign bond yields were never seriously affected. Nevertheless, Sarkozy clearly faced external pressure to adopt a more Ordoliberal stance. At the same time, however, the President faced domestic resistance to more liberal economic policies.

4. Methods

The changes in the leaders' economic policy ideas will be established by applying the technique of CCM (Van Esch 2012; Axelrod 1976; Young 1996; Young and Schafer 1998). The maps constructed in this study are composed on the basis of leaders' public speeches concerning European economic and monetary issues. In order to create a cognitive map, all causal and utility relationships alluded to by a leader are manually derived from a text.[1] Utility statements are statements to the effect that something is 'good', 'in someone's interest' or 'in the general benefit'. To make comparison possible, terms with similar meanings are pooled under overarching, merged concepts (Laukkanen 2008). Finally, leaders' worldviews are represented as a graphic map in which the standardised concepts are depicted as points and the relations between these concepts as arrows (see Figure 1).[2] To facilitate this process, CCM software Worldview and Gephi were used (Young 1996).

For every leader, a cognitive map was constructed for the period prior to the outbreak of the crisis (CM[1]) and for the first two years after the onset of the Euro-crisis (CM[2]).[3] Ideational changes may also have taken place within the boundaries of these timeframes. However, since a significant amount of data is needed to construct maps that do justice to the full width of leaders' worldviews, two broad time periods were selected. This made it

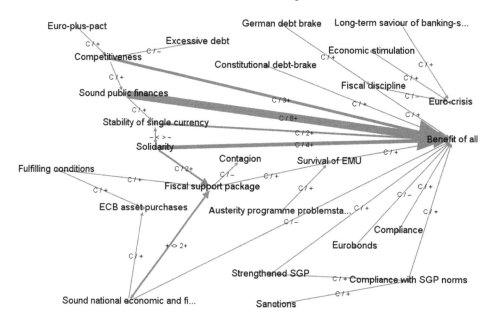

Figure 1. Merkel's views on Euro-crisis management (excerpt from CM[2]).

possible to base the maps on speeches directed at various audiences and increase the construct-validity of the maps.

To establish the extent to which leaders adhere to Keynesian or Ordoliberal thought, all standardised concepts were classified as Keynesian, Ordoliberal or neutral and the aggregated 'saliency' per paradigm is calculated.[4] Saliency (S) is the frequency with which concepts or relations are mentioned. In addition, a qualitative analysis of the CMs as a whole was conducted to establish whether, and to what extent it included causal and normative paths (sequences of concepts and relations) that represent ideal typical Ordoliberal or Keynesian rationales. Subsequently, leaders' pre-crisis and crisis CMs were compared to establish whether leaders experienced *stability*, a *reversal, reduction* or *reinforcement* of pre-crisis ideas. Moreover, comparison of leaders' ideas over time and across person will show whether the crisis fostered ideational convergence or divergence.

The use of public sources in this study enables the analysis of high political leaders' ideas on a contemporary issue such as the Euro-crisis. However, it does raise the question of the nature of the ideas reflected in the maps. First, it is important to stress that this study does not necessarily aim to reveal leaders' private ideas. The selected leaders are of interest primarily because of their public role in the management of the Euro-crisis and their private convictions are mainly of interest when they are publicly acted upon via speech-acts or behaviour. However, nor do the maps necessarily display 'genuine' or deeply internalised ideas. While several studies have indicated that leaders' public speeches of leaders provide an adequate approximation of the trends in more privately held beliefs (Axelrod 1976; Marfleet 2000; Renshon 2009; but see Hay and Smith 2010), ideas are also often used strategically (Hay and Smith 2010; Schmidt 2008). Moreover, political psychologists have shown wide variation in the extent with which political leaders actually internalise beliefs (Keller 2009). The definite verdict of whether this study taps into strategic or internalised ideas will therefore be out until (more) private sources become available.

However, the CM technique offers some clues as to the extent in which leaders' publicly espoused ideas were strategic or internalised. First, internalised ideas are by nature more stable than strategic beliefs in light of external pressures for adjustment. As such, the level and intensity of changes uncovered may indicate the type of ideas tapped into. In addition, the technique offers two distinct levels of analysis: the quantitative analysis reveals what concepts are part of leaders' claims and their saliency. These scores may be expected to rise when leaders reference strategically to particular topics in their speeches. The underlying logic (or network of relations) in leaders' argumentation is less susceptible to such strategic manipulation. In fact, CM was developed precisely to reveal the hidden (faulty) assumptions and rationale in decision-makers logic that they are themselves unaware of (Axelrod 1976). It is precisely with the aim to strip a rationale back to its bare structure that the speeches are reduced to graphs. Large disparities between the outcomes of the first- and the second-order analysis may therefore be a second indicator of a more strategic use of ideas.

5. Angela Merkel: Madam-Non Turns Maybe?

The first important finding concerning the views of Angela Merkel emerges from the search for speeches. Prior to the outbreak of the Euro-crisis, the Chancellor makes few references to European integration and hardly mentions European economic and monetary integration. The onset of the crisis significantly increases Merkel's references to the EU as well as EMU and the Euro (Boin, 't Hart, and Van Esch 2012). These references reveal that prior to the crisis, Merkel had a strong Ordoliberal outlook on economic and monetary policy-making. The overall saliency of Ordoliberal concepts (19% of the total map saliency) was eight times as high as that of Keynesian concepts (2.3%).

The qualitative analysis mirrors this image, for while the Chancellor did not engage in any detailed economic analysis, her CM reveals two strains of text-book Ordoliberal logic. To begin with, the ECB should first and foremost serve the goal of price stability (S = 7) and its independence was seen as a necessary condition for sound single monetary policy-making, the credibility and stability of EMU. In addition, Merkel applauded the SGP for stimulating sound national economic policy and public finances. The only remarkable exception to the Ordoliberal character of her views is that the consequences Merkel attributed to EMU were largely Keynesian in nature.

While after the onset of the crisis, Merkel remains Ordoliberal in her thinking—with Ordoliberal twice as salient as Keynesian views—some significant changes did occur. First, the Ordoliberal character of her map has reduced. This is caused by the near complete omission of her monetary strain of reasoning: Key Ordoliberal concepts like ECB independence (S = 1) and price stability (S = 3) become significantly less salient. Simultaneously, reflecting the prevailing European discourse at the time, fiscal arguments become dominant in the Chancellor's mind. The majority of these—such as her pleas for the strengthening of the SGP (S = 5), constitutional debt-brakes (two concepts, S = 3, 1) and fiscal discipline (S = 8)—are clearly Ordoliberal. However, Merkel also refers favourably to several Keynesian crisis-measures such as the fiscal support packages (S = 12), conditional ECB-interventions (both S = 3) and the Euro-plus-pact (S = 1) as means to foster positive evaluated goals like the survival of the EMU, restoration of market trust (both S = 10) and competitiveness (S = 18). Overall, Merkel's views remain predominantly Ordoliberal, but a significant reduction in the paradigmatic orthodoxy of her ideas takes place.

6. Axel Weber, the Ordoliberal Hawk

The policy ideas of the German Bundesbank President Axel Weber show a different pattern. First, the analysis shows that Weber's pre-crisis economic beliefs were stringently Ordoliberal, they make up a whopping 37.1% of the aggregate map saliency, while references to more Keynesian values and measures only make up 5.2% (see Figure 2).

A more in-depth analysis of the Bundesbank President's map provides further evidence of his orthodox Ordoliberal ideas: prior to the crisis, the classic Ordoliberal value of price stability is by far the most salient concept (S = 28). Moreover, the ECB's policies should be geared towards the goal of price-stability to serve the general benefit (S = 18), sound single monetary policy (S = 8) and the success and stability of EMU (S = 12, 5). In addition, Weber adheres to the classic Ordoliberal belief that monetary policy should be conducted independently from politics (S = 4) and shows a strong concern for sound public finances (S = 6) and fiscal discipline (S = 4). This is reflected in his views on the European response to financial crisis: while Weber is positive about the effects of the ECB measures to liquidise the markets (S = 6), he perceives too much

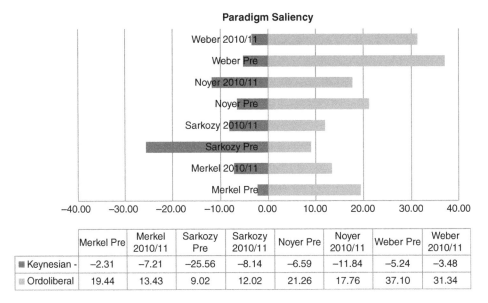

	Merkel Pre	Merkel 2010/11	Sarkozy Pre	Sarkozy 2010/11	Noyer Pre	Noyer 2010/11	Weber Pre	Weber 2010/11
■ Keynesian -	−2.31	−7.21	−25.56	−8.14	−6.59	−11.84	−5.24	−3.48
▨ Ordoliberal	19.44	13.43	9.02	12.02	21.26	17.76	37.10	31.34

Figure 2. Aggregate saliency of Keynesian and Ordoliberal concepts.

liquidity (S = 4) and the bank bailouts (S = 3) as a threat to price stability and fiscal discipline. Only under exceptional circumstances and strict conditions should such interventions occur.

The outbreak of Euro-zone crisis is shown to reinforce Weber's Ordoliberal views. While the overall saliency of both his Keynesian and Ordoliberal ideas drop slightly to 31.3% and 3.5%, the relative dominance of Ordoliberal views increases (from factor 7.1 to 9.0). The in-depth qualitative analysis does, however, reveal some interesting crisis-induced changes. First, a shift is evident from a focus on monetary to fiscal issues. Concepts such as sound public finances (S = 28), fiscal discipline (S = 8) and excessive deficit (S = 7) multiply both in number and saliency. Weber's views on proper monetary policy-making and ECB autonomy do not change, but the saliency of concepts such as 'price stability' (S = 14) drops significantly. Weber—like Merkel—thus perceives the Euro-crisis essentially to be a public debt crisis. This is mirrored in his preferred solutions to the crisis (see Figure 3): Weber advocates strongly Ordoliberal measures such as strengthening of the SGP (three concepts, S = 7, 6, 4), enforced compliance (S = 2) and a debt brake. Fiscal support measures (S = 11) are met with less enthusiasm, for while Weber acknowledges that these measures fostered financial stability (S = 8) and provide the necessary liquidity (S = 8), he also perceives them to be contradictory to the foundations of EMU (S = 4) and detrimental to the success of EMU. As for crisis-interventions by the ECB, his pre-crisis concerns are amplified. More than ever, Weber feels that the ECB assets and liquidity measures should be strictly conditional (S = 9) and temporary (S = 8) so as not to endanger the stability of the Euro and financial system by increasing liquidity and price stability beyond acceptable levels. Overall, the policy ideas of the former Bundesbank President are thus not only strongly Ordoliberal but also highly stable in face of the crisis. In fact, the onset of the Euro-crisis reinforces his pre-existing policy ideas.

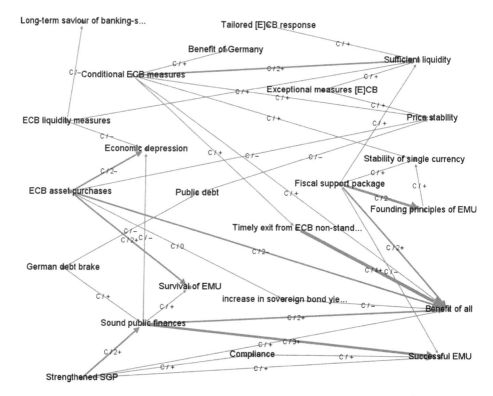

Figure 3. Weber's views on Euro-crisis management (excerpt from CM²).

7. Sarkozy's Partial Paradigm Shift

The pre-crisis cognitive map of President Sarkozy was largely Keynesian in character. The saliency of his Keynesian ideas was 2.8 times as high as that of his Ordoliberal views (see Figure 2). The qualitative analysis shows, however, that while the President's ideas were clearly in defiance of Ordoliberalism, his views lack several orthodox Keynesian elements.

Prior to the crisis, the President's main line of thinking revolved around his conviction that monetary and exchange rate policy should be governed by politicians ($S = 18, S = 19$) rather than central banks. To make this possible, a European economic government ($S = 12$)—a meeting of the European Heads of State and Government—should be established. This would foster economic growth and employment, promote the national interest and help solve the financial crisis. In the eyes of the President, such government is not at odds with the independence of the ECB ($S = 8$): a conviction clearly in contradiction to the Ordoliberal paradigm. However, his main motivation for placing European monetary and exchange rate policy in the hands of politicians was to nullify the competitive advantage of low exchange rates of other world powers, and counter the 'monetary dumping' by the USA. Arguments that are more mercantilist than Keynesian. In addition, Sarkozy did not advocate classic Keynesian measures like government expenditure and investment but did support the flexibilisation of the SGP. In sum, Sarkozy's pre-crisis views were clearly not Ordoliberal, but simultaneously low in Keynesian orthodoxy.

With the outbreak of the crisis, Sarkozy experienced a paradigmatic reversal in views. As a result of a significant reduction of Keynesian ideas, his Ordoliberal views became dominant. An in-depth analysis of his underlying rationale reveals a more ambiguous picture (see Figure 4). First, after the onset of the Euro-crisis, Sarkozy develops more fiscal ideas and explicitly voices the Ordoliberal opinion that poor public finances lay at the root of the Euro-crisis. In his eyes, sound public finances (S = 7) and the (strengthening of) SGP (S = 6) are necessary for the credibility and success of EMU, while government expenditure (S = 1) and public debt (S = 5) endanger national independence. At the same time, however, the President advocated Keynesian measures such as the establishment of a European monetary fund (S = 3), fiscal support (S = 6) and the Euro-plus-pact (S = 3). In monetary terms, Sarkozy's crisis beliefs remain in conflict with Ordoliberal thinking. Although the two dominant arguments pleading for political use of monetary and exchange rate policy disappear as such, Sarkozy still deems high exchange rates (S = 6), speculation (S = 6) and monetary dumping by the USA (S = 1) as problematic and the establishment of a 'European economic government' (S = 8) conditional for the success of EMU. All in all, the onset of the Euro-crisis induces a paradigm reversal in the President's ideas from Keynesian to Ordoliberal. This reversal seems to be somewhat superficial, never fully influencing his underlying rationale, and only concerns the fiscal dimension of his worldview.

8. Christian Noyer: Crisis-Induced Ambiguity

The ideas of French central bank director, Christian Noyer, also underwent a significant change. Quantitative analysis shows that, prior to the crisis, his ideas were predominantly

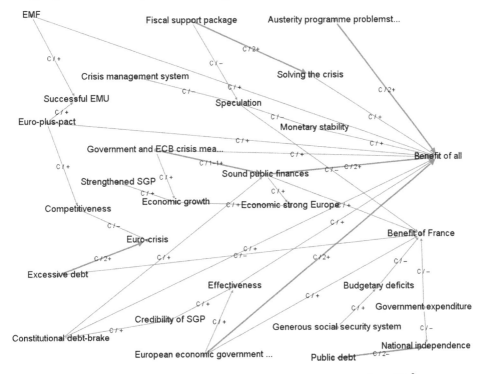

Figure 4. Sarkozy's views on Euro-crisis management (excerpt from CM^2).

Ordoliberal (21.3% vs. 6.6%). The qualitative analysis of Noyer's pre-crisis cognitive map supports this view: price stability is by far the most salient goal (S = 26), while more Keynesian goals such as employment (S = 5) and economic growth (S = 3) rank much lower. Moreover, prior to the crisis, Noyer firmly rejects expansionary monetary policy (two concepts, S = 7, 4) and denounces expanding the mandate of the ECB beyond guarding price stability (five concepts, S = 5, 3, 2, 2, 1). Moreover, he reiterates the traditional Ordoliberal view that ECB independence promotes price stability which in turn has no negative effect on employment. Finally, prior to the crisis, Noyer advocates sound public finances (S = 5) and fiscal discipline (S = 3) as means to increase price stability. He also talks favourably about investment (S = 3), cohesion policy (S = 2) and financial transfers (S = 2) within the EU, policies that are more Keynesian in character. These, however, rank lower in terms of saliency.

After the crisis, this balance changes but falls short of complete paradigmatic reversal: while the overall saliency of his Ordoliberal views drops only slightly to 17.8%, the saliency of his Keynesian beliefs increases from 6.6 to 11.8 (see Figure 2). Qualitative analysis of the map shows this to be caused by a drop in the saliency of the concept price stability (S = 1) and disappearance of the issue of ECB independence and mandate. Moreover, there is a decrease in the overall number and saliency of concepts referring to monetary issue while the number and saliency of fiscal concepts increases dramatically. As for the causes of the crisis, Noyer recognises the detrimental effects of the 2008 financial crisis on the national debts and deficits. However, he perceives the Euro-crisis as a problem of market trust (S = 18) and its negative effect on government bond yields (see Figure 5).

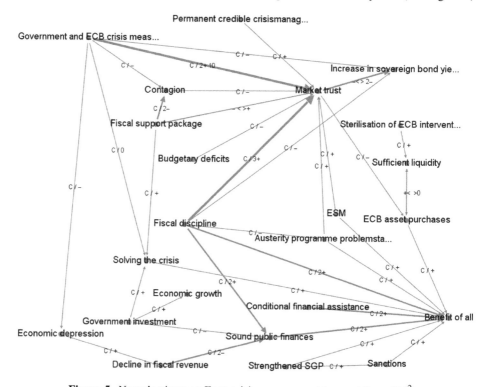

Figure 5. Noyer's views on Euro-crisis management (excerpt from CM^2).

Of the 23 crisis measures he identifies, most are fiscal in nature and diverse in terms of the Ordoliberal and Keynes paradigms: calls for austerity and conditionality of support are more numerous but Keynesian measures—like ECB asset purchases (S = 10) and fiscal support packages (S = 8)—are more salient. Overall, with the onset of the crisis, Noyer thus becomes more ambiguous in his economic views with Keynesian ideas gaining ground. These changes, however, fall short of a complete paradigmatic reversal and only amount to a weakening of pre-existing Ordoliberal ideas.

9. Conclusions

This study aimed to uncover to what extent a paradigmatic divide existed between key French and German decision makers, and to what extent the outbreak of the Euro-crisis caused a change and convergence in their views. From the analysis it is clear that prior to the crisis, the leaders under study adhered to different policy paradigms. However, leaders' policy ideas prove to be far more ambiguous and flexible than the ideal-typical paradigms. Moreover, the divide amongst them is not as wide as often is assumed, nor does it neatly follow national borders. Surely, the German leaders had more stringently Ordoliberal ideas, but the views of the French central bank governor, Noyer, also fell within the Ordoliberal domain. Only Sarkozy's pre-crisis ideas on monetary issues were of a more Keynesian nature.

In addition, the outbreak of the crisis shows that leaders' policy views were far more susceptible to change than the idea of a competing paradigm would suggest. First, all leaders were open to current affairs and bore witness of this in their thoughts. They differed, however, to the extent in which their pre-existing ideas determined their evaluation of these current affairs lending support to the thesis that both crisis-learning and threat-rigidity occur empirically. Weber was most consistent and uncompromising in his views, evaluating every aspect of the Euro-crisis through the lens of his stringent Ordoliberal views. Merkel, Noyer and Sarkozy's policy ideas were more malleable: with the onset of the crisis, Sarkozy experiences a reversal in ideas in the fiscal realm and Noyer starts advocating Keynesian crisis measures. Merkel is the most stable of the three, but also incorporates several new Keynesian lines of thinking in her argumentation.

In addition to underscoring the point that leaders' ideas are more ambiguous and flexible than the ideal-typical paradigms, leaders' views thus also show some convergence. First, a clear meeting of minds takes place on the definition of the Euro-crisis: all leaders define the Euro-crisis as a 'sovereign debt' crisis and thereby conform to the prevailing European discourse of the day. Moreover, the ideas of Merkel, Sarkozy and Noyer also show some paradigmatic convergence: with the onset of the crisis, they all move towards a modestly Ordoliberal position. The reinforcement of Weber's ideas thus places him further away from the average position and contrary to the expectations of the epistemic community literature, convergence is less prominent amongst the central bankers than the political leaders. Most remarkably, however, is the fact that on average the leaders move away from the strong traditional Ordoliberal stance of the dominant partner, Germany. This raises questions about the hegemonic role of Germany in European affairs as well as the place of the French–German axis therein.

However, this brings us back to the fundamental question of what this public display of discursive convergence means. For, the study also clearly shows that the changes and convergence uncovered are more pronounced in terms of the concepts leaders use than their underlying rationale. This is especially true for the French President, the most pressured leader. As indicated before, the distinct pattern of change he displays—paradigmatic reversal that is grounded only superficially in his underlying rationale—may be indicative of a strategic use of ideas. While his discursive shift—heartfelt or not—will have influenced and have facilitated, a lack of internalisation of ideas by political leaders may in the long-run prove detrimental for the sustainability of the policy-decisions they facilitate (Van Esch and De Jong 2013). However, now that we have a clearer and more nuanced view of leaders' economic ideas, future research may shed light on these questions and further our understanding of how leaders' views may influence European decision-making.

Notes

[1] For the CM coding rules, see Bonham and Shapiro (1986) and Wrightson (1976). Deriving causal maps from documents have been shown to come natural and intercoder reliability amongst experienced coders to be high (Axelrod 1976; Young and Schafer 1998).

[2] In a CM positive (C/+), negative (C/−) and non-existing (C/0) relations are distinguished. Bi-directional relations between concepts are indicated by $<\ >$, the saliency of a relation by the number in the arrow. As the figures in this paper are excerpts, the concepts may have additional links not displayed.

[3] The speeches date from 18 January 2006 to 27 May 2009 and from 23 February 2010 to 16 September 2011 with exception of one 2002 speech by Noyer's selected to achieve a sufficient inclusive map. Each map consists of 65–168 unique relations.

[4] With help from an economist not involved in the study, a coding manual was constructed for the paradigms. Independent coding by two raters (including the author) returned a 'substantial' Cohen's Kappa of 0.73 (Gwet 2012, 122–128). For the few remaining differences between the raters and the expert after consultation, the assessment of the author was used.

References

Axelrod, R. 1976. *Structure of Decision. The Cognitive Maps of Political Elites*. Princeton, NJ: Princeton University Press.

Beyers, J. 2005. "Multiple Embeddedness and Socialization in Europe: The Case of Council Officials." *International Organization* 59 (4): 899–936.

Blyth, M. M. 1997. "'Any More Bright Ideas?' The Ideational Turn of Comparative Political Economy." *Comparative Politics* 29 (2): 229–250.

Blyth, M. M. 2013. *Austerity: The History of a Dangerous Idea*. Oxford: Oxford University Press.

Boin, A., P. 't Hart, and F. A. W. J. Van Esch. 2012. "Political Leadership in Times of Crisis: Comparing Leader Responses to Financial Turbulence." In *Comparative Political Leadership*, edited by L. Helms, 119–141. Basingstoke: Palgrave Macmillan.

Bonham, G. M., and M. G. Shapiro. 1986. "Appendix 2: Coding Instructions for the CM Procedure." In *Different Text Analysis Procedures for the Study of Decision Making*, edited by I. N. Galhofer, W. E. Saris, and M. Marianne, 125–139. Amsterdam: Sociometric Research Foundation.

Burnell, P., and A. Reeve. 1984. "Persuasion As a Political Concept." *British Journal of Political Science* 14 (4): 393–410.

Carstensen, M. B. 2011. "Paradigm Man Vs. the Bricoleur: Bricolage As an Alternative Vision of Agency in Ideational Change." *European Political Science Review* 3 (1): 147–167.

Checkel, J. T. 2001. "Why Comply? Social Learning and European Identity Change." *International Organization* 55 (3): 553–588.

Deverell, E. 2009. "Crises As Learning Triggers: Exploring a Conceptual Framework of Crisis-Induced Learning." *Journal of Contingencies and Crisis Management* 17 (3): 179–188.

Dullien, S., and U. Guerot. 2012. "The Long Schadow of Ordoliberalism: Germany's Approach to the Euro-Crisis." *European Council on Foreign Affairs. Policy Brief*, no. 49: 1–16.

Dyson, K. H., and K. Featherstone. 1999. *The Road to Maastricht. Negotiating Economic and Monetary union*. Oxford: Oxford University Press.

Goldstein, J., and R. O. Keohane. 1993. *Ideas and Foreign Policy: Beliefs, Institutions, and Political Change*. Ithaca: Cornell University Press.

Gwet, K. L. 2012. *Handbook of Inter-Rater Reliability*. Gaithersburg, MD: Advanced Analytics, LCC.

Hall, P. A. 1993. "Policy Paradigms, Social Learning, and the State: The Case of Economic Policymaking in Britain." *Comparative Politics* 25 (3): 275–296.

Hall, P. A. 2012. "The Economics and Politics of the Euro-Crisis." *German Politics* 21 (4): 355–371.

Hay, C., and N. Smith. 2010. "How Policy-Makers (Really) Understand Globalization: The Internal Architecture of Anglophone Globalisation Discourse in Europe." *Public Administration* 88 (4): 903–927.

Howarth, D., and C. Rommerskirchen. 2013. "A Panacea for All Times? The German Stability Culture As Strategic Political Source." *West European Politics* 36 (4): 750–770.

Kaelberer, M. 2002. "Ideas, Interests, and Institutions: The Domestic Politics of European Monetary Cooperation." *Comparative Politics* 35 (1): 105–123.

Keller, J. W. 2009. "Explaining Rigidity and Pragmatism in Political Leaders: A General Theory and a Plausibility Test from the Reagan Presidency." *Political Psychology* 30 (3): 465–498.

Krotz, U., and J. Schild. 2012. *Shaping Europe. France, Germany, and Embedded Bilateralism from the Elysée Treaty to Twenty-First Century Politics*. Oxford: Oxford University Press.

Laukkanen, M. 2008. *Comparative Causal Mapping with CMAP3. A Method Introduction to Comparative Causal Mapping and a User's Manual for CMAP3*. Kuopio: Kuopio University Occasional Reports H. Business and Information Technology 2.

Levy, J. S. 1994. "Learning and Foreign Policy: Sweeping a Conceptual Minefield." *International Organization* 48 (2): 279–312.

Marcussen, M. 1999. "The Dynamics of EMU Ideas." *Cooperation and Conflict* 34 (4): 383–411.

Marfleet, B. G. 2000. "The Operational Code of John F. Kennedy During the Cuban Middle Crisis: A Comparison of Public and Private Rhetoric." *Political Psychology* 21 (3): 545–558.

McNamara, K. R. 1998. *The Currency of Ideas: Monetary Politics in the European Union*. New York: Cornell University Press.

Parsons, G. 2002. "Showing Ideas As Causes: The Origin of the European Union." *International Organization* 56 (1): 47–84.

Renshon, J. 2008. "Stability and Change in Belief Systems: The Operational Code of George W. Bush from Governor to Second Term President." *Journal of Conflict Resolution* 52 (6): 820–849.

Renshon, J. 2009. "When Public Statements Reveal Private Beliefs: Assessing Operational Codes at a Distance." *Political Psychology* 30 (4): 649–661.

Sabatier, P. A., and H. C. Jenkins-Smith. 1993. *Policy Change and Learning: An Advocacy Coalition Approach*. Boulder, CO: Westview Press.

Schmidt, V. A. 2008. "Discursive Institutionalism: The Explanatory Power of Ideas and Discourse." *Annual Review of Political Science* 11: 303–326.

Schmidt, V. A. 2010. "Taking Ideas and Discourse Seriously: Explaining Change Through Discursive Institutionalism As the Fourth 'New Institutionalism'." *European Political Science Review* 2 (1): 1–25.

Segers, M. L. L., and F. A. W. J. Van Esch. 2007. "Behind the Veil of Budgetary Discipline: The Political Logic of the Budgetary Rules in EMU and SGP." *Journal of Common Market Studies* 45 (5): 1089–1109.

Staw, B. M., L. E. Sandelands, and J. E. Dutton. 1981. "Threat Rigidity Effects in Organizational Behavior: A Multilevel Analysis." *Administrative Science Quarterly* 26 (4): 501–524.

Steinbruner, J. D. 1974. *The Cybernetic Theory of Decision: New Dimensions of Political Analysis*. Princeton, NJ: Princeton University Press.

Stern, E., and B. Sundelius. 1997. "Sweden's Twin Monetary Crises of 1992: Rigidity and Learning in Crisis Decision Making." *Journal of Contingencies and Crisis Management* 5 (1): 32–48.

Van Esch, F. A. W. J. 2007. "Mapping the Road to Maastricht. A Comparative Study of German and French Pivotal Decision Makers' Preferences concerning the Establishment of a European Monetary Union during the early 1970s and late 1980s." Unpublished Phd. Thesis. Nijmegen: Radboud University Nijmegen, Faculty of Management Sciences.

Van Esch, F. A. W. J. 2012. "Why Germany Wanted EMU. The Role of Helmut Kohl's Belief-System and the Fall of the Berlin Wall." *German Politics* 21 (1): 34–52.

Van Esch, F. A. W. J. and E. De Jong 2013. "Institutionalisation without Internalisation.The Cultural Dimension of French-German Conflicts on European Central Bank." *International Economics and Economic Policy* 10 (4): 631–648.

Verdun, A. 1999. "The Role of the Delors Committee in the Creation of EMU: An Epistemic Community?" *Journal of European Public Policy* 6 (2): 308–328.

Wincott, D. 2004. "Policy Change and Discourse in Europe: Can de EU make a 'Square Meal Out of a Stew of Paradox'?" *West European Politics* 27 (2): 37–41.

Wrightson, M. T. 1976. "The Documentary Coding Method." In *Structure of Decision. The Cognitive Maps of Poltiical Elites*, edited by R. Axelrod, 291–332. Princeton, NJ: Princeton University Press.

Young, M. D. 1996. "Cognitive Mapping Meets Semantic Networks." *The Journal of Conflict Resolution* 40 (3): 395–414.

Young, M. D., and M. Schafer. 1998. "Is There Method to Our Madness? Ways of Assessing Cognition in International Relations." *Mershon International Studies Review* 42 (1): 63–96.

From the Maastricht Treaty to Post-crisis EMU: The ECB and Germany as Drivers of Change

ARIE KRAMPF

Academic College of Tel Aviv-Yaffo, Israel

ABSTRACT   *The Eurozone crisis brought the European Economic and Monetary Union (EMU) to the brink of collapse; the prevention of this required the use of unconventional measures by the European Central Bank (ECB), the construction of new financial regulatory institutions, and an amendment of EMU laws. These changes culminated in the establishment of a banking union, though not a complete one. This article has two aims. First, it seeks to evaluate to what extent the European crisis management strategy led to a fundamental change in the EMU institutional design. Second, it seeks to identify the key drivers of change, with a focus on the interaction between ECB, the Commission, and Germany.*

1. Introduction

The Eurozone crisis brought the European Economic and Monetary Union (EMU) to the brink of collapse; the prevention of this required the use of unconventional measures by the European Central Bank (ECB), the construction of new financial regulatory institutions, and an amendment of EMU laws. These changes culminated in the establishment of a banking union, though not a complete one, which shared risks among European countries. While there is agreement that the response to the crisis changed the EMU, there is no agreement on whether these changes should be considered 'patches' added to the existing institutional framework of the EMU, or as a more fundamental change in the EMU institutional design.

The question regarding the policy drift within the EMU also has political repercussions. The EMU was shaped primarily by German preferences. Germany's position regarding the structure of the EMU was dictated by two key objectives: maintaining a zone of stable exchange rates, and shifting the burden of adjustment to the high inflation European countries (Moravcsik 1998; Moravcsik and Schimmelfennig 2003). The crisis management strategy that included risk sharing, therefore, went counter to the German pre-crisis preferences. The question arises, therefore, what the factors that led Germany to change its position regarding the European crisis management strategy were.

The article, therefore, has two aims. First, it seeks to evaluate to what extent the European crisis management strategy breached pre-crisis EMU principles. Second, it seeks to identify the causes that led Germany to make concessions and accept, at a later stage of the crisis, proposals that it rejected at an earlier stage. In order to address these questions, I first identify four pre-crisis EMU policy principles. Then, in Section 3, I trace the ECB's policy instruments used throughout the crisis, the discourse used to legitimize these policies and the new institutions that were established in the institutional vicinity of the ECB. The analysis will examine to what extent these policies breached pre-crisis EMU policy principles. In Section 4 I trace the bailout agreements in order to determine the drift in the German position regarding the crisis management strategy and how it was linked to the ECB's policies. Finally, I discuss the factors that may explain why Germany changed its position.

2. Pre-crisis EMU Policy Principles

The EMU did not include a crisis management mechanism. When the crisis hit the European countries, European policy-makers had to devise new policy instruments and establish new institutions to address the crisis. To what extent did these changes affect the institutional design of the EMU? Among scholars there is no agreement regarding this question. For Salines and others the response to the crisis was only a 'temporary redirection' of the EMU, in which the 'ultimate objective' remained unchanged (Salines, Glöckler, and Truchlewski 2012, 668). Braun argues that the response to the crisis left imprints on the 'ideational and institutional landscape' of the EU, but was the product of experimentation and bricolage rather than of a paradigm change (Braun 2013, 2).

Others suggest that the response to the crisis led to a more fundamental change. Baker suggests that the EMU shifted from the 'old Basel consensus' on micro-prudential regulation to a 'new but incomplete' consensus on macro-prudential policies (Baker 2013, 119). Along the same lines, Quaglina identifies a shift from 'Old' to 'New' politics of financial services regulation in the EU. While the Old politics was 'market making' the New one was 'market shaping' (Quaglia 2012; see also Quaglia 2011). The insider, Jürgen Stark, identified a shift to a 'new normal' in central banking (Stark 2011).

In order to evaluate the extent to which the response to the crisis affected the institutional design of the EMU, in this section I identify four pre-crisis EMU policy principles. The four principles will serve as points of reference for the analysis of the European crisis management strategy.

Policy principles are discursive entities which are less abstract than paradigms or ideas but are more general than concrete policy directives. Policy principles are not identified by what actors say they believe in, but rather they are manifested in the practices of actors. Policy principles may thus be viewed as belief-driven acts (Seabrooke 2007, 252). Acts, in our case, also include speech acts, i.e. declarations, announcements, and statutes by governing actors. Therefore, reports, statutes, and other type of formal documents are all instances of belief-driven speech acts, from which we can extract policy principles. Therefore, in order to extract the pre-crisis EMU policy principles, I have analyzed EMU and EU statutes and reports produced in relation to the establishment of the EMU (Delors 1989; Maastricht 1992; Lisbon 2007; EC 1997).

In the *monetary policy area*, the institutional design of the EMU was based on a clear separation between monetary and fiscal authorities. This separation was legitimized in the orthodox theory of the quantitative theory of money and also in the German Ordo-liberal legacy. In countries which are not part of a currency union, this separation is achieved by establishing an independent central bank endowed with a mandate to pursue price stability. In the European currency union, the separation was institutionalized in addition by delegating the monetary power to the European level, while leaving the fiscal powers at the national level (Delors 1989; Maastricht 1992).

In the *fiscal policy area*, the EMU imposed fiscal discipline on member states through EU legislation. During the 1990s, the capacity of the EU to impose fiscal rules was strengthened by the stability and growth pact. The member states had to 'abide by the medium-term budgetary objective of positions close to balance or in surplus' (EC 1997). Moreover, the Lisbon Treaty and the stability and growth pact included policy rules under the heading of 'economic coordination' that significantly restricted the fiscal flexibility of the member states. The stability and growth pact also enhanced surveillance over structural policies concerning labor, product, and services markets.

The designers of the EMU did not pay much attention to the *financial regulation* policy area. By default, they left financial regulation at the national level. This institutional structure was legitimized via the micro-prudential regulation approach, which was reflected in the Basel II accord (Begg 2009). This 'old' Basel consensus (Baker 2013) assumed a separation between monetary and supervisory authorities. The separation ensured that the central bank would be committed to its primary objective of price stability, and would not be distracted from this objective by issues of financial stability.

The fourth pre-crisis EMU principle is the most general and the most important: the prohibition on *intra-European transfer of resources and risks*. The Lisbon Treaty (article 125) includes the much discussed 'no bailout clause' stating that the EU shall 'not be liable for or assume the commitments … of any Member State' (Lisbon 2007). This principle was essential from the perspective of Germany and the high credit-rated countries as it prevented the moral hazard problem in the structure of the EMU and strengthened the EU's capacity to impose sound money policies and fiscal discipline on its members. Hence, according to the pre-crisis EMU policy principles, if the transfer of resources is to take place within the EU, it has to be subjected to the laws of the market, based on extra-EMU agreements among autonomous political and economic units (Table 1).

When the crisis broke out, the question European institutions and member states faced was whether the crisis could be resolved without breaching the pre-crisis EMU

Table 1. Pre-crisis EMU policy principles

Policy area	Policy principles
Monetary	Separation between monetary and fiscal authorities
	Single objective of price stability
Fiscal	EU-level directives of fiscal discipline
Financial regulation	Micro-prudential regulation (Basel II)
	Separation between monetary authority and banking supervisory authority
	No need for European-level regulatory agency
Cross-national transfer of resources and risks	Prohibition of cross-national allocation of resources and risks

Source: author

policy principles. In the earlier stages of the crisis, the German government, with the vocal support of the Bundesbank, as well as the Netherlands and Finland, adopted the view that the crisis could be resolved by using the bailout agreement to impose fiscal discipline, sound money policies, and structural reform in exchange for liquidity. They even proposed the establishment of a fiscal union—delegating fiscal powers to the European level. However, as the political feasibility of a fully fledged fiscal union was meager, other European actors—the ECB and Commission, as well as France, Italy and Spain—promoted the establishment of a banking union without delegation of fiscal authority.

In this article, I trace how, during the crisis, from May 2010 till March 2014, a policy drift took place within the EMU, during which the ECB and the Commission's strategy won out over the German strategy. The aim of the article is to trace this process and explain why Germany succumbed to the approach of the European technocrats.

3. ECB: Policies, Discourse and Institutions

3.1 Policies

Trichet used the term 'non-standard measures' for the first time in September 2008 when the ECB expanded its balance sheet by 150%. It was a modest expansion in comparison to those undertaken by the Fed and the Bank of England (Figure 1). Simultaneously, the ECB lending interest rate was reduced from 5.25%, in July 2008, to 1.5% by the end of the year (ECB 2009, 32, chart A). Another policy instrument used by the ECB at that early stage of the crisis was the *Covered Bond Purchase Programme* (CBPP1), which was announced in May 2009. The CBPP was designed to address the problem of the high spread of the

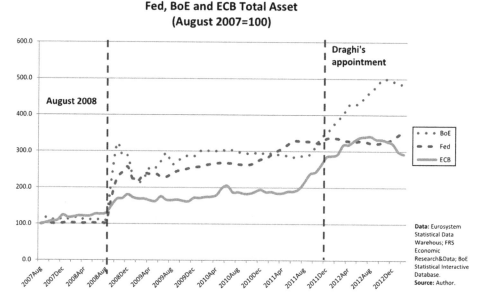

Figure 1. Fed, Boe and ECB total asset (August 2007 = 100).

covered bonds swaps of European banks. The rise was steepest in Ireland (Beirne et al. 2011, 19 chart 5).

When the crisis eventually hit the European periphery and Greece signed the first bailout agreement in May 2010, the ECB supplemented the European response through intervention in the public and private debt security markets with the Securities Markets Programme (SMP). The SMP was designed for the purchase of both private and public debt instruments in order 'to ensure depth and liquidity in those market segments that are dysfunctional' (ECB 2010).

Trichet was very careful to emphasize that the ECB would not step outside its mandate. He explained that 'Price stability is our primary mandate' (Trichet 2010a) and that the purpose of the non-standard measures was to 'promote the ongoing decline in money market term rates, to encourage banks to maintain and expand their lending to clients' and they were in fact a necessary repair to the 'transmission system' of the monetary policy (Trichet 2009).

Unlike the Bundesbank, Trichet thought that a decisive and unconventional response was needed, but he also believed that the responsibility for devising this response should lie with the political echelon. The crisis, he argued, should be addressed by 'supra-national institutions and laws as well as the international relations between countries that have an effect on cross-border economic and financial transactions' (Trichet 2010c).

The turning point in the ECB approach to the crisis took place after Mario Draghi succeeded Trichet as President of the ECB in November 2011. Prior to becoming President, Draghi had served as a chairman of the Financial Stability Board, an international institution established by the G20 after the Asian financial crisis to promote global financial stability. His previous position may explain Draghi's sources of legitimacy and his bold position regarding unconventional ECB policies.

Soon after his appointment, Draghi announced the so-called 'Big Bazooka', the *long-term refinancing operation* (LTRO). In fact, the LTRO was not new in the ECB arsenal. The LTRO was a conventional refinancing instrument. What turned it into a 'Big Bazooka' was that the ECB extended the loan term from one month to three years at a favorable interest rate (1%); the ECB also expanded the type of assets that could be used as collateral. The LTRO, therefore, enabled banks to get rid of bad assets, including government bonds, and replace them with solid assets (Pattipeilohy et al. 2013). In December 2011, the ECB lent €490 billion to 523 banks and in February 2012 an additional €530 billion to 800 banks.

A significant aspect of the LTRO was the geographical distribution of the loans. In fact, this was used a risk sharing instrument by which the ECB took upon itself the risk from the infected countries. In the early stages of the crisis (August 2008 to September 2010), the main beneficiary of the LTRO was Germany: it was used to minimize the exposure of German banks to infected banking systems. From November 2011, the total volume of the LTRO expanded by 250% and its main beneficiaries were Spain, Italy, France and Portugal (Figure 2). This geographical pattern implies that the LTRO breached the pre-crisis principle prohibiting the intra-European transfer of risks and resources.

The LTRO was a game changer in the ECB's management of the crisis as it addressed two problems simultaneously: it improved the stability of the banking system by replacing short- with long-term liabilities, and it eased the sovereign debt crisis, absorbing a portion of the sovereign bonds in the market and thereby reducing the long-term interest rates (Praet 2012). In March 2012, the value of the three-year loans made by the Eurosystem to European banks was estimated at around €1 trillion (Atkins 2012).

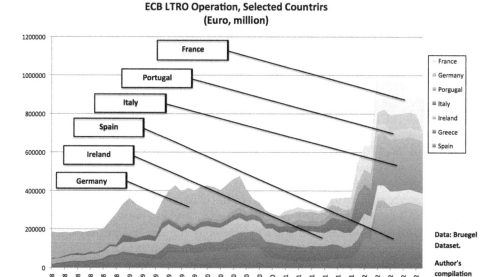

Figure 2. ECB LTRO operation, selected countries.

Another important ECB instrument was *outright monetary transactions* (OMT), which was a program for purchasing government bonds at one- to three-year maturities for countries ready to accept conditionality criteria (Draghi and Constâncio 2012). The Governing Council of the ECB announced the establishment of the program in August 2012, two months after the Euro summit in June, to which we will return. As of April 2014, the OMT has not been used. However, it had two major implications. First, it shaped market expectations regarding the willingness of the ECB to do 'whatever it takes' to save the Euro. Second, the OMT has become an element of the European Stability Mechanism (ESM), which is a bailout mechanism.

3.2 Discourse

The ECB policies were legitimized by a new approach to financial regulation called 'macro-prudential policies'. The extensive resources dedicated to developing the approach supports the claim that the non-standard measures were not a form of bricolage but a more fundamental change in the design of the EMU.

The notion of macro-prudential policies emerged for the first time in the context of the Bank of International Settlements (BIS) following the Asian crisis (Baker 2013). However, it became a buzzword after it was adopted by key international financial institutions following the sub-prime crisis. The prestigious Group of 30 promoted a more integrated approach to financial regulation in its report from 2008 (G30 2008). In 2009, the International Monetary Fund, the BIS and the Financial Stability Board (which Draghi chaired) prepared a report on the causes of financial instability, in which they highlighted the systemic causes of it (IMF, BIS, and FSB 2009).

In 2008, the president of the European Commission, José Manuel Barroso, appointed Jacques de Larosière, who was also a member in the Group of 30, to chair the *Independent High Level Group on Financial Supervision* to reconsider the European regulatory framework. The group published a report in early 2009 in which it set out a 'new regulatory agenda' for monetary policy-making and financial regulation. The report was highly critical of the regulatory norms prior to the crisis: the 'Basel 1 framework did not cater adequately for, and in fact encouraged, pushing risk taking off balance-sheets. This has been partly corrected by the Basel 2 framework' (de Larosière 2009, 9). 'Regulators and supervisors focused on the micro-prudential supervision of individual financial institutions and not sufficiently on the macro-systemic risks of a contagion of correlated horizontal shocks' (de Larosière 2009, 10).

De Larosière's report highlighted the role of market confidence in financial stability. It quoted a report prepared by the G30 saying that market confidence, which is

> taken for granted in well-functioning financial systems, has been lost in the present crisis in substantial part due to its recent complexity and opacity… weak credit standards, mis-judged maturity mismatches, wildly excessive use of leverage on and off-balance sheet, gaps in regulatory oversight, accounting and risk management practices that exaggerated cycles, a flawed system of credit ratings and weakness of governance. (G30 2009, 15)

On the basis of the American experience, the report recommended the establishment of a European System of Financial Supervisors (EFSF); this would include a set of financial supervision agencies that would contribute to 'burden sharing' within the Eurozone (de Larosière 2009, 35). These institutions were the seeds of the banking union.

Following the publication of the report in September 2010, Trichet declared the establishment of the Macroprudential Research Network (MaRs) (Trichet 2010b). The MaRs was an extensive project involving more than 180 researchers from all EU national central banks and the ECB, who were working on 126 individual projects and two joint cross-country projects involving multiple central banks. The research carried out by the MaRs reached the conclusion that a financial system may be locked in a 'crisis equilibrium', which is a situation in which 'financial agents ("banks") lose confidence in other financial agents ("banks") to whom they lend', which is caused by 'widespread endogenous imbalances' (ECB 2012, 16). In order to address this problem, an active approach to financial regulation was needed.

3.3 Institutions

On November 2009 the Commission announced the establishment of four European financial supervisory agencies: the European Securities and Markets Authority (ESMA), the European Banking Authority (EBA), the European Insurance and Occupational Pensions Authority (EIOPA), and the European Systemic Risk Board (ESRB). The new framework was called the European System of Financial Supervision (ESFS) (Figure 3).

The establishment of the four European Supervisory Agencies did not require amendment of EMU law as it used the legislation procedure of the Commission. The downside of this was that these agencies did not have binding powers on governments and could only make recommendations and rely on their normative power (EBA 2010; EIOPA 2010; ESMA

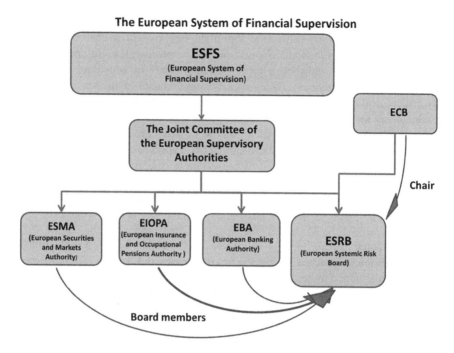

Figure 3. The European system of financial supervision.
Source: Author illustration

2010; ESRB 2010). Nevertheless, the powers that the new regulatory framework had were enhanced by its links with the ESM and the ECB (Figure 4). According to the ESM guidelines, the four regulatory institutions participate in the implementation and monitoring of the bailout programs, together with the ECB (Wyplosz, Gros, and Belke 2011).

4. Germany and the Bundesbank: Bailout Agreements

The ECB policies faced fierce criticism from the Deutsche Bundesbank. Its president, Axel Weber (until April 2011), rejected the ECB interpretation according to which the crisis was caused by 'domestic factors within the deficit countries,' rather than by systemic factors. Therefore, 'it is mainly incumbent on them [the deficit countries] to act' (Weber 2010). The ECB, claimed Weber, should focus on its 'primary objective ... defined as a stabilization of the inflation rate at around 2% across a horizon of approximately two years.' The instrument for achieving this goal was 'steering short-term interest rates' (Weber 2011). According to the Bundesbank, the crisis should be solved by imposing 'credible consolidation of public finances' and 'improvements in economic governance in EMU that ensure prudent fiscal policies in the medium to long run,' as Andreas Dombert, a member of the Executive Board (Dombert 2011), explained. In the early stages of the crisis, Merkel and Schäuble followed the Bundesbank approach and pushed for very strict conditions in exchange for rescue packages. When the ECB and the Commission proposed the establishment of a single supervision mechanism (SSM) and a single resolution mechanism (SRM), Germany responded by arguing that it would accept these institutions only if they were be accompanied by a fiscal union, in which 'nation states give up their

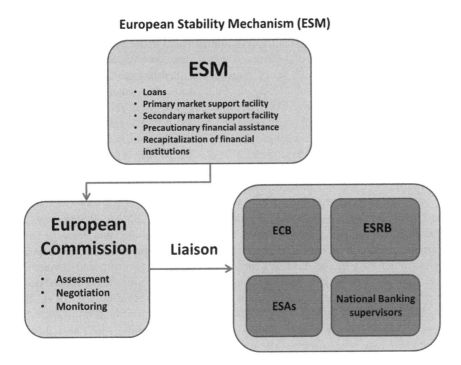

Figure 4. European stability mechanism (Euro million).
Source: Author illustration

jurisdiction in terms of fiscal policy,' as Schäuble put it. 'As long as we don't have a fiscal union, we cannot assume joint liability for debts.'[1]

However, despite the rhetoric, Germany made several concessions. The first sign of change was the amendment to Article 125 of the Lisbon Treaty and the introduction of Article 136 of the Treaty on the Functioning of the European Union, which allowed for the establishment of an ESM (EC 2011a). By July 2011, most member countries had signed up to the amendment.

In July 2011, when Greece signed its second bailout package, the Commission declared that the Greek agreement 'will be designed, notably through lower interest rates and extended maturities, to decisively improve the debt sustainability and refinancing profile of Greece.' As for the EFSF and the ESM, the Commission also announced its intent to 'increase their flexibility linked to appropriate conditionality' in order 'improve the effectiveness of the EFSF and of the ESM and address contagion.' For that purpose, the EFSF (and the ESM) would be allowed to take precautionary measures to recapitalize financial institutions (through loans to governments) and to intervene in the secondary markets (EC 2011b). These amendments were institutionalized in the ESM once the 'no bailout' clause was amended (ESM 2012, articles 14–18).

The most significant concession, however, was made by Germany at the Euro summit of 29 June 2012. During the summit, Merkel faced pressure from Monti and Rajoy, the Italian and Spanish prime ministers, regarding the terms under which Spanish banks would be recapitulated. According to news reports, after a long night of negotiation, Merkel caved in and accepted their demands.[2]

Merkel made three concessions that were implemented in the Spanish bailout package. First, conditionality was eased and interest rates were lowered. Second, the ESM was allowed to recapitalize Spanish banks directly and therefore no structural reform was demanded from the government. Finally, the ECB received a greater role in the process in its capacity to purchase bonds (EU Council 2012). The press release stated that 'it is imperative to break the vicious circle between banks and sovereigns' and made reference to the SSM: 'When an effective single supervisory mechanism is established, involving the ECB, for banks in the euro area the ESM could, following a regular decision, have the possibility to recapitalize banks directly' (EU Council 2012).

The German concessions in June paved the way for the establishment of the banking union. In September, the three triple-A rated European countries—Germany, the Netherlands and Finland—endorsed the establishment of the SSM (Joint Statement 2012), defined as the 'first leg of a banking union'. The legislation stated that the large banking institutions in Europe would be supervised by the ECB and the European regulatory agencies, rather than by the more lenient national agencies (Barroso and Barnier 2013; also see Howarth and Quaglia 2013). In March 2014, a compromise was achieved between Germany, the Commission, and the other governments regarding the SRM. In the compromise, Germany agreed to pool resources at the European level via the SRM. However, the resources would be levied from the banks themselves (rather than from governments) and the process of recapitalization would be authorized by an intergovernmental agreement, which would provide Germany with significant powers (EC 2014). The proposal of a SRM was hailed by rating agencies, who claimed that it would be 'positive for investor confidence in Eurozone sovereigns.'[3]

5. Drivers of Change

Judging on the basis of outcomes, during the period from May 2010 to March 2014, Germany made significant concessions. Most importantly, Germany accepted the idea of sharing risks and debt without a delegation of fiscal powers. In order to explain this drift, I consider here two alternative explanations: either Germany succumbed to external pressure or it recalculated its preferences.

Germany was, and is, by far the most powerful European economy. Therefore, other European member countries or European institutions have no material leverage over Germany. However, as a regional leader and due to the unique historical background to European integration, Germany is very anxious to ensure that it is perceived in the EU as a benign leader. Until the crisis, the German position regarding the design of the EMU enjoyed the support of the economic experts and the technocrats from Brussels (Verdun 1999). This support contributed to German legitimacy as a European leader; following the crisis, Germany was accused of acting as a European hegemon and the conflict with the economic experts in Brussels did not help Germany to deal with these accusations.[4] As a result, the EU institutions were able to exert 'normative power' over Germany.

During 2011, the confrontation between Germany and the Commission escalated. Barroso believed that Merkel's vision of a 'two speed Europe' was intended to strengthen the intergovernmental European institutions at the expense of the Commission. He ridiculed it, arguing that the intergovernmental institutions allowed 'a few idiots' in one country to 'blackmail' the entire EU.[5] At the same time, Draghi publicly expressed his lack of confidence in the ability of the EFSF and the ESM, with their limited capacities, to resolve the crisis. These institutions, he argued, 'fell short' of what Europe needed (Draghi 2012). The ECB sought to extend the power of the ESM and turn into a lender of last resort by broadening its powers to 'intervene in secondary government bond markets in order to effectively combat contagion in situations of acute market instability' (ECB 2011, 77).

The public campaign of the ECB and the Commission culminated in a report prepared by the two presidents, in collaboration with Herman Van Rompuy, the president of the European Council, and Jean-Claude Juncker, the president of the Eurogroup, just prior to the June 2012 summit. The report, entitled *Toward a Genuine Economic and Monetary Union* (Van Rompuy et al. 2012), presented a new 'vision' for the EMU and called for the construction of a banking union. The report of the 'Gang of Four' received significant attention from the international media. The Bloomberg Newsweek presented it as an EU Roadmap to a Fiscal and Banking Union (Neuger and Christie 2012).

Germany must have faced difficulties in dealing with the discreditization of its proposal by the ECB and the Commission. However, Germany also had a domestic interest in changing its position on the crisis management strategy. The turning point in the German position occurred when the crisis reached Spain. The Spanish economy is eight times larger than the Irish economy, five and half times larger than the Portuguese, and four and a half times larger than the Greek.[6] Moreover, the German and French banks were highly exposed to Spanish and Italian banks. The exposure of the German banks to Italian and Spanish banks (combined) was more than 10%, whereas their exposure to Greek and Portuguese and Irish banks (combined) was less than 6%. The case of France was shakier: the debt of Spanish and Italian banks to French banks amounted to almost 16% of their foreign assets, whereas the debt of Irish, Greek, and Portuguese banks to French banks was less than 3% (Table 2).

The relatively small size of Greece, Portugal, and Ireland, and the low level of exposure on the part of the German and French banks, increased the German negotiation power vis-à-vis these countries. Germany could make a credible threat to let these countries default. Indeed, Schäuble actually made such a threat in the case of Greece.[7] Spain and Italy, however, were 'too big to fail' and Germany faced a huge risk if the rescue package was postponed. From March 2012, the long-term rates of Italian and Spanish bonds rose above 5%. In June 2012, just before the summit, Moody's downgraded Spain to Baa3, just

Table 2. Exposure of German and French banks to European peripheral banking systems (2012 Q1)

Country	Germany		France	
	US$ Mi	**(%)**	**US$ Mi**	**(%)**
Greece	26.6	1.1	36.7	1.2
Ireland	93.8	3.5	37.2	1.2
Italy	133.5	4.9	346.6	11.5
Portugal	27.2	1.0	20.3	0.7
Spain	139.9	5.2	127.9	4.3
All countries	2706.7	100.0	3007.6	100.0

Notes: The BIS consolidated banking statistics on an immediate borrower basis (CIBL_IB) track consolidated foreign claims of banks headquartered in individual reporting countries and for the reporting area as a whole. The data are from the creditor perspective, and thus can be used to track the foreign exposures of banking systems to countries and sectors on an immediate borrower basis. *Source*: BIS statistics.

a notch above speculative asset, and Italy to Baa2, one notch higher.[8] The same month, Moody's downgraded the rating of six large German banks due to the 'increased risk of further shocks emanating from the euro area debt crisis.'[9]

The exposure of Germany and France to the debt crisis changed the situation for Merkel and Schäuble and forced them to recalculate German preferences. Germany did not abandon its preference for fiscal discipline, but the importance of this objective was overcome by the more urgent objective of keeping the Eurozone together. The spillover of the crisis to Spain and Italy increased the odds of a Eurozone collapse and Germany had to accept the ECB's crisis management strategy.

6. Conclusion

The Eurozone crisis caught the EMU unprepared and European policy-makers, at the national and European level, had to devise a strategy to address the crisis. Throughout the crisis, two competing strategies emerged. Germany and the high credit-rated economies promoted a strategy which highlighted the need for fiscal discipline, sound money policies, and structural reforms. This strategy was consistent with the pre-crisis EMU policy principles and did not require deep institutional change. It only required the establishment of a European liquidity fund as well as the improvement of the EMU to impose fiscal discipline by establishing a fiscal union.

On the other hand, the ECB and the Commission, as well as France, Spain, and Italy, pushed for a strategy which highlighted the financial systemic failures that led to loss of market confidence. According to this approach, fiscal soundness is important but is far from sufficient to resolve the crisis. The approach assumed that the resolution of the crisis required policy instruments that involved sharing risks and resources, such as a SSM and a SRM. In short, it opted for the establishment of a banking union.

The two strategies did not contradict each other, but they differed significantly in terms of emphasis and sequencing. Germany was willing to accept a banking union only if European governments were willing to delegate fiscal powers to the European level. This proposal was highly unrealistic and in practice blocked the Commission proposal for a SSM and SRM. The ECB and the Commission pushed for the establishment of a banking union, even without a fiscal union.

In the earlier stages of the crisis, the two strategies were employed simultaneously as a reasonably effective, second best solution: the ECB non-standard measures were used as an ad hoc lender of last resort, preventing the banking systems of infected countries from collapsing and governments from defaulting; the bailout agreements were used to impose fiscal discipline and structural reforms, while providing governments with access to a credit line.

As the crisis deepened and spilled over to Spain and Italy, the pressure for a more coherent strategy mounted. Financial markets were not impressed by the bailout agreements and market confidence continued to deteriorate. Furthermore, as the ECB took upon itself more risk by purchasing sovereign bonds, its capacity to address future crises weakened. The Euro summit of June 2012 was the turning point: Germany made serious concessions and in fact adopted, with some exceptions, the crisis management strategy of the ECB.

The European crisis management strategy, as shaped by the ECB and the Commission, breached three of the four pre-crisis principles outlined above. First, and most importantly, the European crisis management strategy breached the prohibition on risk and debt sharing as the ECB, via the LTRO, took risk upon itself from the infected countries and collectivized it. Moreover, the compromise on the establishment of a SSM and a SRM is based on pooled resources, which could be activated without intergovernmental agreement.

Second, while the pre-crisis principle of micro-prudential regulation implied a separation between the monetary and supervisory agencies, the SSM increased the coordination between the two agencies and made the ECB responsible for large banking institutions in Europe.

Third, the establishment of the banking union indirectly affects the separation between monetary and fiscal issues and therefore weakens the capacity of the ECB to commit to the objective of price stability. As the president of the ECB is becoming responsible for a large number of policy goals, under the general heading of financial stability, the organization's capacity to commit to the single objective of price stability is weakened in practice even if no actual amendment to the ECB mandate is made. Moreover, as the ECB is not responsible for financial stability broadly defined, it has now to take into account the long-term rates of sovereign bonds. Therefore, the new institutional design blurs the separation between monetary and fiscal issues. The only pre-crisis EMU principle that has not been affected by the crisis is the one that refers to the EMU fiscal discipline. Despite debates on the preferred crisis management strategy, there has been a consensus among European policy-makers that member states have to abide by the austerity policies.

The analysis raises questions about whether the new institutional structure of the EMU is an intermediate stage in the path of Europe to a fiscal union, as Germany has envisioned, or whether that is a second best institution that might put EMU on a new path of integration, which is more aligned with the French vision. Are we witnessing the emergence of a new consensus between Brussels, Paris, Madrid, and Rome or a disintegration of the Brussels-Frankfurt consensus? Time will tell.

Acknowledgements

This article is based on research conducted during my stay at the KFG 'The Transformative Power of Europe' at the Freie Universität, Berlin, directed by Prof. Tanja Börzel and Prof. Thomas Risse. An earlier version of the paper was presented at the Research Seminar of the KFG and I would like to thank Prof. Fritz Scharpf for his valuable comments. I also thank Dr Ali Arbia, Dr Benjamin Braun, and Dr Doris Wydra, for reading and commenting on earlier versions.

Notes

[1] *Spiegel Online*, June 25, 2012.
[2] *Spiegel Online*, June 29, 2012; *BBC*, News Europe, June 29, 2012.
[3] Fitch Ratings, 12 July, 2012.
[4] *EU-Observer*, 'No German "hegemony" in Europe, Merkel says', April 22, 2013.
[5] *Spiegel Online*. May 9, 2011.
[6] OECD StatExtracts http://stats.oecd.org/.
[7] *Spiegel Online*, September 12, 2011.
[8] Moody's website, https://www.moodys.com.
[9] Moody's website, https://www.moodys.com.

References

Atkins, R. 2012. "Bundesbank Steps up Pressure on Draghi." *Financial Times*, March 13.
Baker, A. 2013. "The New Political Economy of the Macroprudential Ideational Shift." *New Political Economy* 18 (1): 112–139.

Barroso, J. M., and M. Barnier. 2013. "Statement Following the European Parliament's Vote on the Creation of the Single Supervisory Mechanism for the Eurozone." MEMO/13/781.

Begg, I. 2009. "Regulation and Supervision of Financial Intermediaries in the EU: The Aftermath of the Financial Crisis." *Journal of Common Market Studies* 47 (5): 1107–1128.

Beirne, J., L. Dalitz, J. Ejsing, M. Grothe, S. Manganelli, F. Monar, B. Sahel, M. Sušec, J. Tapking, and T. Vong. 2011. "The Impact of the Eurosystem's Covered Bond Purchase Programme on the Primary and Secondary Markets." ECB Occasional Paper, no. 122.

Braun, B. 2013. "Preparedness, Crisis Management and Policy Change: The Euro Area at the Critical Juncture of 2008–2013." *The British Journal of Politics & International Relations*. http://onlinelibrary.wiley.com/doi/10.1111/1467-856X.12026/abstract

De Larosière, J. 2009. *High Level Expert Group on EU Financial Supervision in the EU*. Brussels: The EU Commission.

Delors, J. 1989. *Report on Economic and Monetary Union in the European Community*. Brussles: Committee for the Study of Economic and Monetary Union.

Dombert, A. 2011. *Securing Financial Stability: The Contribution of Economic Policy. Speech at the New Year's Reception of Deutsches Aktieninstitut*. Brussels: Deutsche Bundesbank.

Draghi, M. 2012. *ECB: Introductory Statement to the Press Conference (with Q&A)*. May 3. Frankfurt am Main: European Central Bank.

Draghi, M., and V. Constâncio. 2012. *Introductory Statement to the Press Conference*. Frankfurt am Main: European Central Bank.

EBA. 2010. *Regulation (EU) No. 1093/2010 of the European Parliament and of the Council Establishing a European Supervisory Authority*. Brussles: European Banking Authority.

EC. 1997. *Resolution of the Amsterdam European Council on the Stability and Growth Pact*. Official Journal C 236 of 02.08.1997 EU Legislation. Amsterdam: European Council.

EC. 2011a. *European Council Decision of 25 March 2011 Amending Article 136 of the Treaty on the Functioning of the European Union*. 2011/199/EU. Brussels: European Council.

EC. 2011b. *Statement by the Heads of State or Government of the Euro Area and EU Institutions*. July 21. Brussels: Council of the European Union.

EC. 2014. *A Comprehensive EU Response to the Financial Crisis: Substantial Progress Towards a Strong Financial Framework for Europe and a Banking Union for the Eurozone*. March 28, Memo. Brussels: European Commission.

ECB. 2009. *Annual Report 2008: The European Central Bank*. Frankfurt am Main: European Central Bank.

ECB. 2010. *Press Release: ECB Decides on Measures to Address Severe Tensions in Financial Markets*. May 10. Frankfurt am Main: European Central Bank.

ECB. 2011. "The European Stability Mechanism." *ECB Monthly Bulletin*, July, 71–84.

ECB. 2012. *Report on the First Two Years of the Macro-Prudential Research Network*. Frankfurt am Main: European Central Bank.

EIOPA. 2010. "Regulation (EU) No 1094/2010 of the European Parliament and of the Council: Establishing a European Supervisory Authority (European Insurance and Occupational Pensions Authority)."

ESM. 2012. "Treaty Establishing the European Stability Mechanism." http://www.esm.europa.eu/pdf/esm_treaty_en.pdf

ESMA. 2010. *Regulation (EU) No 1095/2010 of the European Parliament and of the Council: Establishing a European Supervisory Authority European Securities and Markets Authority*. Brussels: European Union.

ESRB. 2010. *Regulation (EU) No 1092/2010 of the European Parliament and of the Council: European Union Macro-Prudential Oversight of the Financial System and Establishing a European Systemic Risk Board*. Brussels: European Union.

EU Council. 2012. "Euro Area Summit Statement." 29 June, 2012. http://pi.gerhardmarold.com/tag/euro/

G30, (Group of Thirty). 2008. *The Structure of Financial Supervision: Approaches and Challenges in a Global Marketplace*. Washington, DC: G30.

G30, (Group of Thirty). 2009. *Financial Reform: A Framework for Financial Stability*. Washington, DC: G30.

Howarth, D., and L. Quaglia. 2013. "Banking Union as Holy Grail: Rebuilding the Single Market in Financial Services, Stabilizing Europe's Banks and 'Completing' Economic and Monetary Union." *Journal of Common Market Studies* 51 (Sep): 103–123.

IMF, BIS, and FSB. 2009. *Report to G20 Finance Ministers and Governors: Guidance to Assess the Systemic Importance of Financial Institutions, Markets and Instruments: Initial Considerations*. International Monetary Fund, Bank of International Settlement, Financial Stability Board.

Joint Statement. 2012. *Joint Statement of the Ministers of Finance of Germany, the Netherlands and Finland*, Accessed August 1, 2014. http://www.vm.fi/vm/en/03_press_releases_and_speeches/01_press_releases/20120925JointS/name.jsp

Lisbon. 2007. "Treaty of Lisbon Amending the Treaty on European Union and the Treaty Establishing the European Community, Signed at Lisbon, 13 December 2007." *Official Journal of the European Union*. 2007/C 306/01.

Maastricht. 1992. *The Maastricht Treaty: Provisions Amending the Treaty Establishing the European Economic Community with a View to Establish The European Community*. Maastricht. Accessed August 1, 2014. http://www.eurotreaties.com/maastrichtec.pdf

Moravcsik, A. 1998. *The Choice for Europe: Social Purpose and State Power from Messina to Maastricht*. Ithaca, NY: Cornell University Press.

Moravcsik, A., and F. Schimmelfennig. 2003. "Liberal Intergovernmentalism." In *European Integration Theory*, edited by Antje Wiener and Thomas Diez, 67–87. Oxford: Oxford University Press.

Neuger, J. G., and R. Christie. 2012. "EU Roadmap to Fiscal, Bank Union Runs Into German Rebuff." *Business Week*, June 26.

Pattipeilohy, C., J. W. Van den End, M. Tabbae, J. Frost, and J. de Haan. 2013. *Unconventional Monetary Policy of the ECB During the Financial Crisis: An Assessment and New Evidence*. DNB Working Paper 381. Amsterdam: De Nederlandsche Bank.

Praet, P. 2012. "Monetary Policy at Crisis Times." Lecture at the International Center for Monetary and Banking Studies. Geneva: European Central Bank.

Quaglia, L. 2011. "The 'Old' and 'New' Political Economy of Hedge Fund Regulation in the European Union." *West European Politics* 34 (4): 665–682.

Quaglia, L. 2012. "The 'Old' and 'New' Politics of Financial Services Regulation in the European Union." *New Political Economy* 17 (4): 515–535.

Salines, M., G. Glöckler, and Z. Truchlewski. 2012. "Existential Crisis, Incremental Response: The Eurozone's Dual Institutional Evolution 2007–2011." *Journal of European Public Policy* 19 (5): 665–681.

Seabrooke, L. 2007. "Legitimacy Gaps in the World Economy: Explaining the Sources of the IMF's Legitimacy Crisis." *International Politics* 44 (2/3): 250–268.

Stark, J. 2011. *ECB: The Global Financial Crisis and the Role of Central Banking*. Frankfurt am Main: European Central Bank.

Trichet, J.-C. 7 May 2009. *ECB: Introductory Statement with Q&A*. Frankfurt am Main: European Central Bank.

Trichet, J.-C. 2010a. *Interview with Handelsblatt*. Handelsblatt, May 12, Translated to English by the ECB.

Trichet, J.-C. 2010b. *Macro-Prudential Regulation as an Approach to Contain Systemic Risk: Economic Foundations, Diagnostic Tools and Policy Instruments*. Speech at the 13th conference of the ECB-CFS Research Network, Frankfurt am Main, September 27.

Trichet, J.-C. 2010c. "Shaping a New World: The Crisis and Global Economic Governance." Lecture at Bocconi University, Milano, April 9.

Van Rompuy, H., J. M. Barroso, J.-C. Juncker, and M. Draghi. 2012. *Towards a Genuine Economic and Monetary Union*. Brussels: European Council.

Verdun, A. 1999. "The Role of the Delors Committee in the Creation of EMU: An Epistemic Community?" *Journal of European Public Policy* 6 (2): 308–328.

Weber, A. A. 2010. *Macroeconomic Imbalances in European Monetary Union: Causes and Policy Challenges*. Speech at the Kangaroo-Group / EPIC Lunch, Strasbourg, September 22.

Weber, A. A. 2011. "Challenges for Monetary Policy in the European Monetary Union." *Federal Reserve Bank of St. Louis Review* 93 (4): 235–242.

Wyplosz, C., D. Gros, and A. Belke. 2011. *The ECB, the EFSF and the ESM – Roles, Relationships and Challenges. Policy Department A: Economic and Scientific Policy*. Brussels: European Parliament.

Enforcing Austerity in Europe: The Structural Deficit as a Policy Target

HUGO RADICE

University of Leeds, UK

ABSTRACT   *In December 2011, the European Council proposed a Fiscal Pact for member states which would impose a binding limit on their structural deficits (SDs), as part of the wider set of measures intended to resolve the Eurozone's sovereign debt crisis. The proposal, adopted by 25 states in the course of 2012–2013, requires that this limit be imposed on each annual budget, with strict rules governing any breaches, subject to sanctions imposed by the Eurozone authorities. The paper examines the economic and political foundations of the measure. It is argued that the SD is meaningless as a policy target, since it is impossible to measure objectively, while politically it reinforces the depoliticisation of economic policy, under which technical experts replace elected governments in managing the national economy. The purpose of the Fiscal Pact is primarily to reassure business and financial élites that there will be no return to the state interventionism and excessive public spending that supposedly characterised the Keynesian era.*

Introduction

In December 2011, more than two years and 20 odd summits into the Eurozone's sovereign debt crisis, the European Commission announced a new Fiscal Pact, designed to ensure that the crisis would never be repeated. The Pact formed part of the wider Treaty on Stability, Coordination and Governance (TSCG), which was signed by 25 European Union (EU) governments in March 2012.[1] Together with other changes such as the revisions to the European Stability Mechanism and the proposals for a European Banking Union, the TSCG has been widely and rightly interpreted as signalling a commitment to austerity for many years to come, and this in turn has helped to galvanise opposition in politics, the media and the street across Europe. It has also been seen as an attack on democracy, given that it transfers powers from elected national parliaments variously to the European Central Bank (ECB) and the European Court of Justice (ECJ) (see e.g. Jennar 2012).

Political economists have provided critical analyses of the Fiscal Pact and the TSCG, such as Sawyer (2013).[2] Mainstream economists have also become more critical, not only of fiscal austerity (e.g. Holland 2012), but also of the Fiscal Pact and the wider TSCG

Originally written for the conference 'The EU after the Crisis' (Weimar, December 2012), later versions of this paper were discussed at the University of Leeds in January 2013 and Roskilde in February 2014.

(e.g. Bird and Mandilaras 2013; Andersen 2013).[3] However, surveying the literature up to the end of 2013, it is clear that the critics are by no means winning the war of ideas. National governments within the Eurozone, having signed the TSCG, are now subject to the full panoply of measures contained in it for policing their fiscal policies. Outside of government, most people have come to accept the neoliberal argument that the fiscal deficit must be 'brought under control', regardless of the social cost: first because public borrowing is bad *per se*, and second because it is the fault of the state not the financial services sector. It is therefore very important for critics to identify the weakest links in the chain of reasoning that is being deployed by the proponents of the Fiscal Pact, as well as by other governments such as the UK Coalition who are, in effect, taking the same approach.

This paper argues that a key starting point for a more penetrating critique is the concept of the structural deficit (SD). At first sight, it seems to be merely a technical change with regard to the deficit target and the means of ensuring the compliance of member states. Clause 4 of the original European Council statement of 9 December 2011 states that the crucial indicator of pact compliance was to be a legally binding SD target of 0.5%, supplementing the limits set by the 1992 Maastricht Treaty (on all EU states), of 3% of GDP for the fiscal deficit and 60% of GDP for outstanding sovereign debt. Although the SD concept has a much longer history within the calculations that underpin fiscal and monetary policy in all the major economies, the EU's Pact marks the first time that it is to play the role of a quantitative target; it is also the first occasion, certainly in the EU, that such a target is to be made legally binding.[4] The aim of this paper is to explore the implications of this for the future character of macroeconomic policy-making in the EZ itself and the world at large. My purpose is to show that it is not only based on a flawed understanding of how the economy works, but also intended to institute a permanent régime of political protection for wealthy élites and austerity for the rest of us.

To these ends, the first half of the paper delves into the economic thinking that underlies the concept and measurement of the SD. This thinking embraces an embarrassingly simple-minded view of the dynamics of capitalism and a barrage of technical sophistry intended to deflect criticism; at its heart stands *homo oeconomicus*, the rational maximising individual of neoclassical economics. The root of the problem concerns how to measure output capacity and growth potential in a modern capitalist economy. The second half of the paper turns to the political purpose underlying the adoption of the SD as the key indicator for the measurement of fiscal sustainability. The argument is based on the concept of 'depoliticisation', that is, the removal of policy decisions from direct control by elected governments in favour of control by allegedly independent agencies. In this regard, the Fiscal Pact accelerates a trend already visible in the EU's Stability and Growth Pact of 1997.

The Economics of the SD

In principle, the SD is a straightforward idea. As one centre-left economist puts it:

> The *structural* deficit is a measure of how large the deficit in public spending would be if the economy were to return to full potential output and then grow at its 'trend' growth rate and stay at that growth rate into the future. The idea of the structural deficit is that it strips out the cyclical effects of recession on the economy—business failures and unemployment—and shows what the fiscal position would be like *if the economy were growing at trend*, averaged over the business cycle. (Reed 2010, 3)

Thus, while the cyclical part of the deficit will cure itself as the economy recovers, a remaining SD (or more precisely, one that fails to meet its current target) signals the need for action to reduce the deficit.

Because the SD cannot be observed from available statistics, estimates are usually based (as Reed implies) upon measurement of the *output gap* (OG), i.e. the difference between actual and potential output at any point in time.[5] The assumption is that, during a recession, the level of the OG will set a ceiling on the extent of the eventual cyclical recovery, and this in turn will set a ceiling on the fiscal outcome. Put briefly, *the bigger the OG, the smaller the SD*; more importantly, *the smaller the OG, the bigger the SD*, and therefore the more fiscal tightening is required to ensure that, when the trend line is reached again, the SD reaches its target level.

However, while the difficulties in measuring *actual* output are mitigated by cross-checking between measures of aggregate sales, expenditure and incomes, it is much harder to determine *potential* output. According to the French group Les économistes atterrés:

> The "structural deficit" is surely one of the most esoteric concepts ever to have figured in an international treaty. It means the fiscal deficit that would occur if a country's GDP was at its full potential ... This approach assumes that it is possible to define a potential growth rate that depends only on supply-side factors (rate of productivity growth, capital stock, active labour force, equilibrium employment rate). In reality the European Commission's method, written into the Treaty, means that its estimate of potential output is always very close to the level actually achieved, particularly in a period of recession. (Les économistes atterrés 2012, 105–106; my translation)

They argue that the supply side factors listed are all dragged down by recession, and go on to show that if, instead, it is assumed that potential output has continued to expand at its average rate, the OG would have been three times greater for France in 2011 than the EC's estimate. The reasons for this downward bias in the estimates of potential output can be explored in the parallel case of the UK.

Traditionally, there have been three main approaches to measuring potential output, and thus the OG (OBR 2011; IFS 2010, ch. 1): statistical filters that mechanically extract a smoothed trend from a time series; using a production function to measure potential output from given measures of inputs and of total factor productivity; and cyclical indicators based on assessments, mostly from surveys, of unused capacity, labour market conditions and productivity trends. In the UK, the third approach was adopted by the Treasury in 2003, and confirmed in HM Treasury (2008). The Office for Budget Responsibility (OBR) initially took over the Treasury method after it was set up by the incoming Coalition government in June 2010 (OBR 2010), but they have since attempted to refine it through a review of alternative approaches (OBR 2011). However, even among UK bodies using the same methodology, for the fiscal year 2009–2010, estimates of the OG varied between -3% and -6% of potential GDP; using the accepted ratio of 0.5 in year 1, such a difference of 3 points would translate into a 1.5 percentage-point difference in the estimate of the SD (IFS 2011, ch. 1, Figs 1.2 and 1.3).[6]

Regardless of the underlying methodology, there has been considerable debate also about the extent to which OG estimates for any given year are revised *through time*. The OECD, which uses a production function method, finds that approach bedevilled by the unreliability of estimates of total factor productivity (Bouis, Cournade, and Christensen 2012); a recent independent study of the same OECD data found that the uncertainty of OG estimates, measured by the extent of their later revision, has actually increased over time despite the best efforts of the statisticians (Chiu and Wieladek 2012).

While the Treasury/OBR method appears more realistic, it is immensely cumbersome, since the approach is based upon listing a large number of potential indicators of spare productive capacity, measuring them (with appropriate statistical testing for the stability of these measures over time) and then assigning weights to these different components (for full details see OBR 2011). Each of these stages involves subjective judgements, and many of the individual measures are themselves based upon business and other surveys in which the respondents are asked to provide their own assessment. As Andersen (2013, 116) puts it, 'It is inherent in the standard method used to assess the CAB[7] that there is substantial uncertainty and noise related to the quantification'; but in addition, we can expect that business predictions will reflect the prioritising of profits over earnings or employment.

The crucial issue concerns whether the measurement of productive potential is accurate. In the UK, Chancellor Osborne has repeatedly argued that the OG has shrunk significantly (and therefore the SD had risen) because the 2008–2009 crisis permanently destroyed productive capacity. As a consequence, the expected recovery would hit the buffers at a point when a substantial (structural) deficit still existed; hence, still more deficit-cutting is required. The first sign of dissent seems to have occurred in the run-up to the 2010 general election, when financial journalist Chris Dillow responded to a famous letter by a group of austerity-supporting economists to the *Sunday Times* (Dillow 2010). But, following the formation of the Coalition government, critical attention focused on the big picture of deficit-cutting and its consequences (Radice 2011).

However, the methodology used to calculate the OG has been subjected to a detailed critique by Bill Martin, published as Martin (2011) and updated as Martin and Rowthorn (2012). These studies argue that the permanent loss of capacity as a result of the crisis was being greatly exaggerated, calling this 'productivity pessimism'. Initially, the OBR analysts had suggested that the crisis had led to the complete closure of productive capacity, notably in the oil and finance sectors, together with a shift from higher- to lower-productivity sectors: Martin (2011) found that these factors could only have a minor impact. More recently, the focus of OBR and similar studies has been instead on the loss of productivity, and of the potential for productivity growth, of employees in post. As Martin and Rowthorn (2012, 6) argue: 'The bone of contention is the amount of spare capacity *within* businesses and their productivity.' Their starting point is a remarkably different pattern of the present cycle after the peak of 2007: the fall in output was twice as large as in the most recent previous cycles, and the recovery only half as large, leading to a GDP level in 2012Q1 that is fully 14.2% below the level if the trend up to 2008Q1 had continued. Yet, the OBR believes that the true OG in 2011 was only − 2.75%, the main cause being the permanent loss in capacity resulting from the crisis, which had offset any additional capacity installed to result in *no growth in capacity* over the last four years.[8]

Martin and Rowthorn (2012) challenge the main arguments behind this productivity pessimism. They argue that measured productivity per worker has declined, and private-sector employment has unexpectedly grown for four reasons. First, businesses have hoarded labour, encouraged by falling real wages; here they note in particular the greater importance today of 'overhead' employees whose services are required regardless of the level of output. Second, there has been a shift to part-time work, which has increased as the recession continues because workers cannot find the full-time work that they seek. Third, low-productivity and low-wage sectors that are not affected directly by stagnant export demand, such as retail and care services, have grown relatively faster. Finally, workers have been increasingly forced by economic necessity into low-productivity and low-earning forms of self-employment. They argue, instead, that low productivity is primarily the result of a lack of aggregate demand in the economy. Their final estimate of the OG is −9.5%, as against a contemporaneous OBR estimate of −2.5% (OBR 2012a, 8). This tallies with other features of the current stagnation: the resilience of company profits and cash reserves, the failure of exports to respond to a falling exchange rate and the inability of British banks to restore the supply of credit. The consequences of this critique for estimating the SD are striking. An OG of −9.5% would imply that the *cyclical* component of the current fiscal deficit is around 6% of GDP; using the March 2012 OBR forecast deficit of 8.3% (OBR 2012a, 5), this would leave the structural component of the deficit at 2.3% of GDP, compared to the OBR forecast of 6.4%.

Finally, it seems likely that the subjective component in the estimation procedure, namely business survey responses, will be pro-cyclical in character. Martin suggests that normal capacity utilisation may be understood by businesses in different ways:

> Normal capacity output may be regarded as a level of output that satisfies businesses' aims, for example, to maximise short-run revenues and profits, or to minimise short-run costs, rather than a level of output that is technologically feasible with existing resources. Such a distinction is frequently drawn in economic studies of firms' capacity. (Martin 2011, 46)

In the context of persistent stagnation of demand, business pessimism may generate an adjustment of estimates of potential output towards the reduced levels of output actually achieved.

In the autumn of 2011, the criticisms of the exaggerated official estimates of the UK's SD appeared to be gaining ground, with two notable articles in the *Financial Times* (Giles 2011; Wolf 2011). There was also a broader shift of opinion, among international agencies as well as academic economists, towards policies of expanding demand, notably through infrastructure investments. To date, however, the UK Chancellor is sticking to the OBR approach, condemning the country to further and deeper deficit cuts. This will ensure further downward pressure on household incomes from falling real wages and cuts in state benefits, and in all likelihood weaker growth in GDP. It is precisely the same fiscal recipe, underpinned by similar official statistical calculations, that will be deployed as the EC's Fiscal Pact is implemented, with similar effects.

The SD and the Politics of Depoliticisation

Politically, the deployment of the SD in the Fiscal Pact continues along the lines established almost from the outset of the ascendancy of neoliberalism, enshrined globally in the Washington Consensus, and regionally in the 1992 Maastricht Treaty and the establishment of the ECB. The overall purpose is to remove the threat perceived by ruling élites of a return to the active national macroeconomic management that is said to have prevailed in the post-war era. In particular, changes in institutions and practices since the mid-late 1970s sought to prevent any further democratic challenge to private wealth and power. Alongside the worldwide assaults on income and wealth taxes, trade union rights and public ownership, neoliberal régimes sought to insulate key policy processes from democratic control. A widespread shift in decision powers from spending departments to ministries of finance was followed up by the adoption of fiscal targeting and by giving central banks independence from parliamentary control. Renewed belief in the natural efficiency of markets became the cornerstone of the supporting economic ideology, which in addition restructured industrial and labour policies around the pursuit of national competitiveness, and supported international freedom of movement for goods and capital, but not (at least for the time being) labour.

In an influential and much-cited paper, Rhodes (1994) argued that UK public sector reforms in the 1980s and 1990s amounted to a 'hollowing out' of the state, consisting of four trends:

(1) Privatisation and limiting the scope and forms of public intervention.
(2) The loss of functions by central and local government departments to alternative service delivery systems (such as agencies).
(3) The loss of functions by British government to EU institutions.
(4) Limiting the discretion of public servants through the new public management, with its emphasis on managerial accountability, and clearer political control through a sharper distinction between politics and administration (Rhodes 1994, 138–139).

Rhodes argued that the result was not simply a reduction in the size of the state, but also a fragmentation of both operational service delivery and responsibility; but for our purposes, the key outcome was a reduction in political manageability and parliamentary accountability.

The fiercest public debates on the issues listed by Rhodes have focused on his first and third trends (privatisation and Europeanisation), while the fourth (new public management) has generated a less well-known but vigorous discussion mainly among accountants and anthropologists (e.g. Power 1997; Strathern 2000). The second issue, the transfer of functions from government departments to ostensibly independent agencies, has been taken up under the rubric of 'depoliticisation'. Kettell (2008, 631) identifies a '... depoliticised form of governance, in which state managers directly relinquish policy control over particular issues, delegating their day-to-day management to ostensibly non-political institutions or rule-based frameworks.' Examples of this in relation to UK macroeconomic policy would include the transfer of monetary policy management from the Treasury to the Bank of England in 1997, and the establishment of the OBR to take over fiscal forecasting, also from the Treasury, in 2010. In the EU, the ECB was established from the outset as independent from the Union's political institutions, while the 1997 Stability and Growth Pact (SGP) entrusted the enforcement of the 1992 Maastricht Treaty debt and deficit limits to the European Commission and the Council of Ministers, in accordance with Rhodes' third element in the hollowing-out of the state. Following breaches of the Maastricht limits by several member states, notably Germany and France, revisions to the SGP in 2005 sought to restore discipline. The 2012 TSCG takes the approach much further, however, because within the Eurozone, the Fiscal Pact entails a transfer of ultimate control over member states' fiscal performance to the ECJ, rather than national parliaments (or indeed the European Parliament). Another more ambiguous and *ad hoc* example of depoliticisation is the assumption of *troika* control in the Eurozone periphery, under which the International Monetary Fund (IMF), the ECB and the European Commission in effect took powers of veto over national fiscal policy as a condition for providing loans.

Mainstream political scholarship interprets depoliticisation within the framework of an ontological antinomy between market and state as modes of distribution and regulation. In democratic forms of capitalism, this translates into electoral choices between alternative economic policy programmes based on different balances between the two, which over time and given path-dependence consolidate into distinctive varieties of capitalism—a variation which can be observed in principle both across countries, and between time periods. In this framework, depoliticisation is the empirical outcome of shifts away from the state taking place at a variety of locations within the institutions of governance.

The difficulty for political scientists lies in identifying the source of these tendencies. In the 'varieties of capitalism' literature, the source is to be found in a range of factors—ideas, technological change, the rise and fall of non-capitalist states and societies—that are essentially held to be *exogenous* to the existing political and social order. In this approach, the primary issue for politics is how to adapt efficiently to such external shocks, and it is usually assumed (explicitly or implicitly) that there are still underlying and shared political values and goals.

However, more than 50 years *before* Rhodes published his paper, Kalecki (1943) had anticipated the consequences for macroeconomic management in a real world in which political values and goals are contested by opposed interest groups. Although the paper is mostly remembered for proposing that a political trade cycle would develop, what is perhaps more striking is that Kalecki straightforwardly identifies the contestation as being between capitalists (referred to mostly as 'business leaders') and workers. He points out that in the 1930s, business leaders opposed state policies aimed at restoring full employment, and sets out the many ways in which the material interests of capitalists and workers stand in direct opposition to each other. Although expressed differently, the pluralist tradition in post-war political sociology adopted a similar approach, seeing political parties as most likely to represent opposing interests.

Within the Marxist tradition, such contestation was a theme of structuralist analysis (e.g. Poulantzas 1973), and is continued more recently by the neo-Gramscian school in international political economy (e.g. Cox 1987; van der Pijl 1998; Gill 2003). Gill (1995) argued that under what he called 'disciplinary neoliberalism', in which the power of capital is exerted through a wide variety of public and private institutions and practices, a 'new constitutionalism' was developing which enshrined the interests of capital in law and in institutions protected from political interference; the approach has since been widely applied to the EU (see e.g. Cafruny and Ryner 2003). An alternative Marxist version of the concept of depoliticisation has been offered by Burnham, one of a group of authors drawing on the 'Open Marxism' tradition.[9] He defines it as ' ... the process of placing at one remove the political character of decision-making' (Burnham 2001, 127). Bonefeld and Burnham (1998) saw the 1997 granting of independence to the Bank of England as the culmination of a longer process in which monetary management was detached from political control, while Bonefeld (2005) applied this approach to the process of European Monetary Union.

The underlying standpoint in these approaches is that there is a contradiction at the heart of how capitalism is constituted, between the two liberal ideals of free market and political democracy. The free market, in its capitalist form, requires the establishment and enforcement of property rights; historically, this entailed a struggle against absolutism, under which property was held only under the authority of the sovereign, and led to the rise of a propertied bourgeoisie. Political democracy, however, implies that the authority of the sovereign is replaced by that of the people as a whole or their representatives. The ascendant bourgeoisie thus required a means whereby the sovereignty of the people would be prevented from interfering with the property rights that they now possessed. This need to limit the scope of democratic politics was not simply a matter of choice or conjuncture; it was and remains a constitutive feature of capitalism as a mode of production.

Importantly, this contradiction is recognised not only by some Marxists, but also by the German ordoliberal school, which flourished in the 1920s–1950s and played an important role in the post-war reconstitution of the Federal Republic of Germany (the 'social market economy'), and is seen by some as the ideological source of contemporary neoliberalism.[10] Bonefeld (2013) identifies as a central ordoliberal concern the tendency of capitalism to generate a propertyless proletariat, which can only protect itself from the fluctuating fortunes of a free market economy by demanding a redistributive state that necessarily encroaches on property rights. Their solution was to make a property-owning democracy viable not by restricting suffrage, as in earlier centuries, but by creating opportunities for all citizens to own property, in other words for the *embourgeoisement* of the workers[11]: they will then identify with the market freedom of the capitalist, and cease to depend upon, or even to support, a redistributive state. In this light, the current course of action being taken by the political élites within the EU cannot be viewed as a response to an essentially exogenous change. Although the financial crisis was initially placed at the door of excessive lending in the US mortgage market in the years up to 2007, the breadth, depth and speed of financial contagion quickly revealed that since the deregulatory wave of the late 1980s and 1990s, European finance had become deeply implicated. The sovereign debt crisis brought forward another external scapegoat, namely the bond markets. The markets—especially by means of the withdrawal of US money market funds from the short-term funding of European banks—demanded the *reallocation of blame* towards the working classes of the Eurozone, the prioritisation of austerity policies and the protection of creditor rights rather than workers' living standards. Faced with this choice, the political élites have made no bones about it: applying the maxim of 'never waste a crisis', they are pursuing the opportunity to effect a major transfer of income and wealth from wage earners to employers. In a Kaleckian or Marxist framework, therefore, austerity policies are in effect an instrument of class war (Radice 2011).

Thus the mechanism of depoliticisation—in the current case of the EU Fiscal Pact, the imposition of a fixed and legally binding limit to the SD—serves to legitimise what is a fundamentally political choice. This legitimation strategy makes use of a range of common-sense public understandings (or misunderstandings): universally, the fear of suffering the same fate as the Greeks, the fear of loss of 'national competitiveness' in world markets and the persistent belief that the public debt is no different from the debt of individual households and businesses. On top of this, there are further elements according to national circumstances: to cite the 'big three' EU states, in Germany the historical fear of inflation; in Britain, the wider Europhobia constantly stirred up by the leading press barons and politicians of the right; and in France, the fear of specifically German competitiveness.

However, the Achilles heel of the depoliticisation strategy is that it rests on the view that matters of economic policy are far too complex to be left to politicians, and that 'the experts' are politically neutral, using their objective knowledge to serve the public interest. It is abundantly clear that the experts currently in charge advance a strategy that serves a particular special interest, that of capital in the guise of 'investors'. The constitutional legitimacy of the EU's package of responses to the crisis has been questioned by Dawson and de Witte (2013); but in any case, the Fiscal Pact's enforcers still have to persuade politicians and the general public that this strategy is indeed in the public interest. During 2013, the EU Commission relaxed fiscal limits in respect of six member states, earning a rebuke from the finance ministries of Germany and Finland for undermining the credibility of the new approach; the EC's Director General for Economic and Financial Affairs replied that fiscal monitoring had to take account of the effects of 'unexpected adverse economic developments', and that this change of approach was 'fairer' (Spiegel 2014; Buti 2014).

Conclusions

Until the 2008–2009 financial crisis, the strategy of depoliticisation was remarkably successful in reshaping the permitted limits of economic policy-making. The breach of those limits during the bank rescues, and the accompanying fiscal stimuli aimed at restoring output and growth, signalled above all to the ruling classes the possible threat of a 'repoliticisation' of economic policy-making. Such a threat appears to be signalled by increasing public discontent with the failure of the present EU régime to deal effectively with the Eurozone crisis. In this light, the 2011 Fiscal Pact proposal, and specifically the clause concerning the use of the SD as a binding target, indicates that the present political élites have no intention of allowing such a strategic shift.

In this paper, I have sought first to challenge the apparent objectivity of the statistical construction of measures of the SD. It turns out that this depends upon the measurement of the gap between present and potential output: this measurement is unreliable because it relies either on mechanical assumptions about economic behaviour that are not realistic (in the case of the statistical filter and production function methods), or alternatively on subjective evaluations based on business surveys overlaid by *ad hoc* aggregation and adjustments (the method used by the UK Treasury and OBR). Critics of these calculations have suggested that the OG is much larger, and therefore the SD much smaller, than the official view. This challenges the supposed need for yet more austerity.

Nevertheless, an argument based solely on the irrationality of economic measurements is by no means a sufficient basis for developing an effective critique of the Fiscal Pact. Nor indeed has it proved effective to campaign against austerity as such, because the present-day public common sense remains resolutely pre-Keynesian. For this reason, it is important to strengthen the case against the Pact by exposing the anti-democratic character of the proposed use of the SD as a policy target, which continues the long-term neoliberal strategy of depoliticising macroeconomic policy-making.

Acknowledgements

For comments and suggestions, I am grateful to the JCES reviewers, and to Henry van Maasakker, Malcolm Sawyer, Bill Martin and Andreas Bieler.

Notes

[1] For details on how the TSCG fits in to the EU's overall economic and financial policy system, see European Commission (2012). For the original official text announcing the pact, see European Council (2011).

[2] See also IMK (2012), the special issue of *Cambridge Journal of Economics* (2013) and the annual reports of the EuroMemorandum Group (e.g. EuroMemo 2013).

[3] See also the special issues of *Journal of Economic Policy Reform* (2013) and *Journal of International Money and Finance* (2013).

[4] The tight fiscal rules introduced in Sweden following the economic crisis of 1991–1993 were not supported by constitutional measures, and thus remained subject to policy discretion (Flodén 2013).

[5] The output gap has also been widely used in relation to monetary policy, where it is seen as setting a limit to monetary stimulus, beyond which it will generate inflationary pressure (see e.g. Bouis et al. 2012, 5).

[6] For details on how the OBR calculates the impact of changes in GDP on the public finances, see OBR (2012b).

[7] Cyclically adjusted balance: an alternative term for the SD.

[8] Martin and Rowthorn (2012) challenge at length the additional contention that in 2007 the UK economy was operating *above* its capacity, with estimates of the OG of up to +6%. Even with a more reasonable +3%, the effect of this on calculations of the 2011 gap is minor.

[9] See Clarke (1991); for a wide-ranging debate between the Open Marxists and the neo-Gramscians, see Bieler et al. (2006).

[10] See also the paper by Young in this special issue.

[11] A phenomenon widely debated in Britain and elsewhere in the 1960s and 1970s (e.g. Goldthorpe et al. 1969), it was embodied in the political strategy of 'popular capitalism' in the UK under Margaret Thatcher, a key example being the sale of council houses to tenants.

References

Andersen, T. M. 2013. "Fiscal Policy Targeting Under Imperfect Information." *Journal of International Money and Finance* 34: 114–130.

Bieler, A., W. Bonefeld, P. Burnham, and A. D. Morton. 2006. *Global Restructuring, State, Capital and Labour: Contesting Neo-Gramscian Perspectives*. London: Palgrave.

Bird, G., and A. Mandilaras. 2013. "Fiscal Imbalances and Output Crises in Europe: Will the Fiscal Compact Help or Hinder?" *Journal of Economic Policy Reform* 16 (1): 1–16.

Bonefeld, W. 2005. "Europe, the Market and the Transformation of Democracy." *Journal of Contemporary European Studies* 13 (1): 93–106.

Bonefeld, W. 2013. "Human Economy and Social Policy: On Ordo-Liberalism and Political Authority." *History of the Human Sciences* 26 (2): 106–125.

Bonefeld, W., and P. Burnham. 1998. "The Politics of Counter Inflationary Credibility in Britain, 1990–1994." *Review of Radical Political Economics* 30 (1): 32–52.

Bouis, R., B. Cournade, and A. K. Christensen. 2012. "Implications of Output Gap Uncertainty in Times of Crisis." OECD Economics Department Working Paper 977, July.

Burnham, P. 2001. "New Labour and the Politics of Depoliticisation." *British Journal of Politics and International Relations* 3 (2): 127–149.

Buti, M. 2014. "The Methodology Behind Budget Targets Is Now Fairer." *Financial Times* letter, March.

Cafruny, A., and M. Ryner, eds. 2003. *A Ruined Fortress? Neoliberal Hegemony and Transformation in Europe*. Lanham, MD: Rowman & Littlefield.

Cambridge Journal of Economics. Special Issue, 37/3: *Prospects for the Eurozone* 2013.

Chiu, A., and T. Wieladek. 2012. "Did Output Gap Measurement Improve over Time?" Bank of England External MPC Unit, Discussion Paper 36, July.

Clarke, S., ed. 1991. *The State Debate*. London: CSE/Macmillan.

Cox, R. W. 1987. *Production, Power and World Order: Social Forces in the Making of History*. New York: Columbia University Press.

Dawson, M., and F. de Witte. 2013. "Constitutional Balance in the EU After the Euro-Crisis." *Modern Law Review* 76 (5): 817–844.

Dillow, C. 2010. "The Myth of the Structural Deficit." *Investors' Chronicle*, February 15. http://www.investors chronicle.co.uk/Columnists/ChrisDillow/article/20100215/1b8f8020-1a1e-11df-b0bd-0015171400aa/The-myth-of-the-structural-deficit.jsp

EuroMemo Group. 2013. *"The Deepening Divisions in Europe and the Need for a Radical Alternative to EU Policies."* http://www2.euromemorandum.eu/uploads/euromemorandum_2014.pdf

European Commission. 2012. *"The European Union Explained: Economic and Monetary Union and the Euro Explained."* Brussels, October. http://europa.eu/pol/emu/flipbook/en/files/economic_and_monetary_union_and_the_euro_en.pdf

European Council. 2011. "Statement by the Euro Area Heads of State or Government." Brussels, December 9 (no longer on line; available from the author).

Flodén, M. 2013. "A Role Model for Fiscal Policy? Experiences from Sweden." *Journal of International Money and Finance* 34: 177–197.

Giles, C. 2011. "The UK Structural Deficit." *Financial Times*, September 19.

Gill, S. 1995. "Globalisation, Market Civilisation and Disciplinary Neoliberalism." *Millennium* 24 (3): 399–423.

Gill, S. 2003. *Power, Resistance and the New World Order.* London: Palgrave.

Goldthorpe, J. H., D. Lockwood, F. Bechhofer, and J. Platt. 1969. *The Affluent Worker in the Class Structure.* Cambridge: Cambridge University Press.

HM Treasury. 2008. *Public Finances and the Cycle.* Treasury Economic Working Paper 5, November. London: HMSO.

Holland, D. 2012. "Less Austerity, More Growth?" National Institute for Economic and Social Research Discussion Paper 400, October.

IFS (Institute for Fiscal Studies). 2010. *The IFS Green Budget: February 2010.* London: IFS.

IFS (Institute for Fiscal Studies). 2011. *The IFS Green Budget: February 2011.* London: IFS.

IMK (Institut für Makroökonomie und Konjunkturforschung). 2012. *Fiscal Pact Deepens Euro Area Crisis.* Report 71e, March. http://www.boeckler.de/pdf/p_imk_report_71e_2012.pdf

Jennar, R. M. 2012. "The Coup in Brussels." *Le Monde Diplomatique (English ed.),* June: 4–5.

Journal of Economic Policy Reform. 2013. Special Issue, 16/1: *Symposium: Policy Dilemmas and the Financial Crisis.*

Journal of International Money and Finance. 2013. Special Issue, 34: *The European Sovereign Debt Crisis: Background and Perspective.*

Kalecki, M. 1943. "Political Aspects of Full Employment." *Political Quarterly* 14 (4): 322–331.

Kettell, S. 2008. "Does Depoliticisation Work? Evidence from Britain's Membership of the Exchange Rate Mechanism, 1990–92." *British Journal of Politics and International Relations* 10 (4): 634–648.

Les économistes atterrés. 2012. *L'Europe mal-traitée: Refuser le Pacte budgetaire et ouvrir d'autres perspectives.* Paris: Les Liens qui Libèrent.

Martin, B. 2011. *Is the British Economy Supply Constrained? A Critique of Productivity Pessimism*, Cambridge: UK Innovation Research Centre/Centre for Business Research, July.

Martin, B., and B. Rowthorn. 2012. *Is the British Economy Supply Constrained II? A Renewed Critique of Productivity Pessimism*, Cambridge: UK Innovation Research Centre/Centre for Business Research, May.

OBR (Office for Budget Responsibility). 2010. *Pre-Budget Forecast: June 2010.* London: HMSO.

OBR (Office for Budget Responsibility). 2011. "Estimating the Output Gap." Briefing Paper 2, April.

OBR (Office for Budget Responsibility). 2012a. *Economic and Fiscal Outlook*, March. London: HMSO.

OBR (Office for Budget Responsibility). 2012b. "Cyclically Adjusting the Public Finances." Working Paper 3, June.

Poulantzas, N. 1973. *Political Power and Social Classes.* London: Verso.

Power, M. 1997. *The Audit Society: Rituals of Verification.* Oxford: Oxford University Press.

Radice, H. 2011. "Cutting Government Deficits: Economic Science or Class War?" *Capital & Class* 35 (1): 125–138.

Reed, H. 2010. *"Rethinking Deficit Reduction."* London: Progressive Economics Panel, June.

Rhodes, R. A. W. 1994. "The Hollowing out of the State: The Changing Nature of the Public Service in Britain." *The Political Quarterly* 65 (2): 138–151.

Sawyer, M. C. 2013. "The Problematic Nature of the Economic and Monetary Union." In *Financial Crisis, Labour Market and Institutions*, edited by S. Fadda and P. Tridico, 79–97. London: Routledge.

Spiegel, P. 2014. "Berlin Attacks EU's Easing of Austerity Demands." *Financial Times*, February 28.

Strathern, M., ed. 2000. *Audit Cultures: Anthropological Studies in Accountability, Ethics and the Academy.* London: Routledge.

van der Pijl, K. 1998. *Transnational Classes and International Relations.* London: Routledge.

Wolf, M. 2011. "Mind the Gap: The Perils of Forecasting Output." *Financial Times*, December 9, 11.

The European Social Model after the crisis: the end of a functionalist fantasy?

CHARLES DANNREUTHER

University of Leeds, Leeds, UK

ABSTRACT   *What is the European Social Model (ESM) for? This paper argues that it is best seen as an ideal type that facilitates the selection of values that sustains the political economy of the European Union. The ESM has facilitated integration in response to changing systemic requirements in the EU: to compensate for Economic and Monetary Union, to coordinate responses to globalisation under the Lisbon Agenda and to offer solace within the EU 2020 agenda after the sovereign debt crisis. As the systemic demands of the EU have changed, the ESM has not. It now has damaging effects on society which have harmed the political integration of the EU. In conclusion, it is argued that the ESM was a missed opportunity, and that while it remains an ideal type rather than a reality, it needs to present a more ambitious political agenda that would reconfirm the EU's commitment to its society over its markets.*

Introduction: the European Union and the crisis

The crisis in the Eurozone has brought about calls for reform in the European Union (EU) as well as in the member states. The Eurozone crisis was the consequence of a sustained series of political choices and strategies at the EU level over the past 30 years that established patterns of inequality and divergence at the national regional and global levels (Aglietta 2012). These were reinforced by the sovereign debt crisis and the European recession (Lapavitsas et al. 2012). As a consequence, all of the Eurozone economies find their economic sovereignty compromised, having submitted to the discipline of the 2012 Treaty on Stability, Coordination and Governance. While the burden of pain has been shared in different ways, fundamental questions relating to EU membership continue to be asked (Zielonka 2014).

At the heart of the compromise built around the introduction of the Euro was the idea of a Social Europe. This was meant to ameliorate the consequences of monetary union on European society as states ceded macroeconomic control to the institutions and procedures of Economic and Monetary Union. The proposal that there were common values in Europe was radical and once the Maastricht Treaty was signed, the Commission set out to find a common set of European values by consulting 'Union institutions, Member States, employers, trade unions and a whole range of other civic institutions, not to mention some individuals' (Commission 1994, 2). The consultation confirmed a set of identifiable values that could underpin what might be called a European Social Model (ESM). These included '...democracy and individual rights, free collective bargaining, the market economy, equality of opportunity for all and social welfare and solidarity' (Commission 1994, 2). These values 'were held together by the conviction that economic and social progress must go hand in hand. Competitiveness and solidarity have both to be taken into account in building a successful Europe for the future' (Commission 1994, 2).

This Maastricht form of EU social policy has clearly failed. Governments are unable to tackle the economic downturns, the single interest rate for the Eurozone prohibits effective ECB intervention, common debt management has been compromised by the no bailout clause and member states have run up significant current account imbalances (Busch et al. 2013). The economic compromise at the heart of the ESM, that 'Competitiveness and social progress [are] two sides of the same coin' (Commission 1994, 3), has in fact led to polarised growth before the crisis (Lapavitsas et al. 2012). In political terms, non-metropolitan voters across Europe have expressed their Euroscepticism in the 2014 European Parliament (EP) elections, as did working class voters, while in key member states the elections confirmed the place of anti-EU political movements in national politics. Since the crisis, the austerity measures designed to improve the competitiveness of especially southern EU member states has radically transformed the prospects of their economies for the worse. If the ESM was unable to offer solidarity when the EU economy was in crisis, what then is its role?

The paper begins by exploring the ESM as an 'ideal type' and assessing how the ambiguity and value bias in such an ideal type have relevance in the framing of European integration. The next section of the paper shows how the ideal type of the ESM enabled functional integration in the EU. It does this by demonstrating how the ESM contributed to greater integration under the Lisbon Agenda than under the EU 2020 and that while these ameliorated initial transformations of the European economy, its effect has subsequently been deleterious. In short, a functionalist explanation of the ESM demonstrates how its impact was more due to changes in the broader economy than the ESM itself.

Governance by ideal type

Ideal types refer 'to the construction of certain elements of reality into a logically precise conception' (Gerth and Wright Mills 2009, 59). They enable comprehension by allowing the observer to better compare forms of behaviour through classifying typologies (Collier et al. 2012, Elman 2005). For Weber, ideal types did not exist in reality nor were they objective or value free. Rather, they were

> ...formed by the one sided accentuation of one or more points of view and by the synthesis of a great many diffuse, discrete, more or less present and occasionally absent concrete individual phenomena, which are arranged according to those one sidedly emphasized view points into a unified analytical construct (*Gedankenbild*). In its conceptual purity, this mental construct (*Gedankenbild*) cannot be found empirically anywhere in reality. It is a utopia. (Weber 1949, 91)

The ideal type was explicitly conceived as an analytical not a practical instrument that would help the historian to determine '...the extent to which this ideal construct approximated to or diverged from reality' (Weber 1949, 91). Case by case, the analyst compared her empirical observations with the value-drenched utopia of an 'ideal type'. In recent years, this form of analysis has been used to good effect by constructivists in public administration (Stout 2010), to demonstrate the nature of EU policies (Forsberg 2011; Rosamond 2014) and to compare national economies (Hancké et al. 2008).

The 'varieties of capitalism' literature demonstrates how complementary activities at the national level enable countries to compete as functional units in a global economy (Hancké et al. 2008). For Becker, these ideal types of capitalism are open systems in the sense that they are 'relatively loosely ordered social entities revealing a certain degree of systemness' (Becker 2009. 22). Importantly, for Becker it ' . . . is not complementary relationships among parts of a political economy that are fundamental but rather the functional relationships of these parts to the political economy's goals or reference frames' (Becker 2007, 268). Institutional complementarities have provided typologies for classifying capitalisms in relation to a wide range of political economy goals like innovation, employment, corporate governance and finance. But Becker's focus on how these relate to the system within which they operate is particularly helpful. This is because it implies that some selection takes place at a systemic level that privileges one form of (for example) labour relationship at the national over another.

Becker's concept of 'reference frame' links institutional complementarity to accumulation in a way that is conceptually similar to a 'mode of social regulation' (MSR) within the Regulation Approach (RA). Both concepts highlight the importance of specifying the elements that need to be analysed in an ideal type, but the MSR tends to focus on institutions. By focusing on 'frames' Becker also highlights the limitations of representing an empirical reality, and captures the potential for political agency better than in the traditional RA approach. The selection of reference frames is central, because rather than being neutral, they reflect a set of values that the coherence of the system as a whole. Institutions do not create realities through complementarities, rather the complementarities are created by the system within which the institutions enable the effective operation of markets.

Through this selection of a reference frame, capitalism creates the realities that reinforce societal relations in ways that are relevant to both time and place (Geras 1971). The ESM offers a clear illustration of how European values privilege property rights overs social rights. A recent review of the ESM found that it enjoyed a wide range of powers and legal capacity (see Table 1). Like much post-Lisbon policy, it relied on soft law alongside hard law in the regulation of markets (Smismans 2011), highlighting the need for a broader analysis that underpinned beliefs and ideas. The ESM also points to the need for discretionary political action at national levels to realise the social agenda, with the Commission providing political support (ter Haar and Copeland 2010). This gap between the legal potential at the EU level and the political practice of the ESM at national levels is what renders it utopian in character.

Indeed, most would concur with the statement that 'to talk about one distinct ESM is in some sense clearly at odds with continued structural and institutional differences between countries' (Montanari et al. 2008, 788). Even calls for a European social policy are couched on the assumption that national compromises should prevail. Scharpf, for example, observes that

> . . . since uniform European social policy is not politically feasible or even desirable, there is reason to search for solutions which must have the character of European

Table 1. The different components of the European Social Model

Hard acquis – found in treaties and EU directives
Health and safety legislation (including working time)
Equal opportunities and anti-discrimination legislation (including a-typical work and temporary agency work)
Mobility of labour including social security rights
Social partner recognition and social dialogue at the EU level
The European Structural Funds, which include the ERDF and the ESF
Soft acquis – associated with the Lisbon Agenda and the OMC
Combating social exclusion by the alleviation of poverty, including active inclusion
European employment strategies (including raising overall employment rates with specific targets for women; development of flexicurity; and active labour market policies)
Extending education and training by lifelong learning
Strengthening social partnership to achieve the objectives of the EES/Lisbon Agenda
Creating long-term sustainable pension systems
Ensuring adequate social protection systems
Improving the reconciliation of work and family life with improved access to childcare provisions
Norms and values – to be found in European Societies
Belief that economic growth should be combined with social cohesion
Comparison of the EU with that of the USA
Belief that an ESM is underpinned by a variety of welfare systems
Belief that the state should provide or at least guarantee public services and services of general interest

Source: ter Haar and Copeland (2010, 281).

law in order to establish constitutional parity with the rules of European economic integration, but which also must be sufficiently differentiated to accommodate the existing diversity of national welfare regimes' (Scharpf 2002, 666).

All of this assumes that the European level has a secondary role compared to the national level in relation to social agendas. Other notions of the ESM appeal to characteristics that are shared by national welfare states. These include a common commitment to social justice that is solidaristic, a cognitive recognition that social justice can contribute to economic growth by reducing uncertainty or as an effective anti-cyclical stabiliser and finally the assertion that there is no contradiction between economic competitiveness and social cohesion (Hemerijck 2002, 174–175).

The ESM has the character of an ideal type, assembled as it is from national welfare systems and from a variety of more or less absent phenomena related to social policy. It is a good example of a 'heuristic device', a tool which has '...proved especially useful in studies of social change, by defining bench-marks, around which variation and differences can then be situated' (Oxford Dictionary 2014). But it has also had a powerful role in legitimating a far weaker set of European measures to counter transnational capital, and a much less rigorous set of ideals for different states to comply with, when compared with macro-economic guidelines.

There is now a large cultural political economy literature that highlights how ideas are performed to assist in the manufacture of realities (e.g. Jessop et al. 2014) that focus on how ideas structure responses and so help generate new realities. Like many other ideas, the ESM enables policy-makers to make sense of the complex world within which they need to make decisions (Jessop 2010). As an ideal type, the ESM has also structured responses to the social problems facing Europe by integrating social and economic interests in the European system on unequal terms. In doing so, it has condemned European social policy to a weak status in the EU's political economy, thereby maintaining the inequalities that plague the EU today.

The ESM and the mythology of functionalism

Functionalism, neofunctionalism and more specifically transactionalism have provided popular explanations for the progression of integration beyond the lowest common denominator of national interests (Deutsch et al. 1957; Haas 1958; Tranholm-Mikkelsen 1991; Stone Sweet and Sandholtz 1997). Functionalist analysis has also linked integration to societal rather than technocratic interests; indeed social policy was one of the case studies that reinvigorated neofunctionalism in the early 1990s (Tranholm-Mikkelsen 1991, 11). For a large part of the late twentieth century, and even the early twenty-first century, the process of technical, political and cultural spillover naturalised the process of European integration. The ESM was linked to a wide variety of meanings and causes (Jepsen and Pascual 2005), including competitiveness (Hyman 2005), flexicurity (Auer 2010), the Open Method of Coordination (van Apeldoorn and Hager 2010), enlargement (Azmanova 2009, Copeland 2012) and the reform of labour markets (Rogowski 2009).

The Lisbon Agenda and EU2020 were themselves responses to different forms of political and economic challenge—the former a period of unparalleled economic growth and political optimism, the latter a response to a crushing economic contraction on a global scale—and the ESM was present in each. The ESM crossed over from the academic category of 'ideal type' into the policy world some time ago. Here, it has become a heuristic device used in policy documents to help define benchmarks against which the integration of member state performance could be evaluated. Presented as an ideal type against which national performance could be compared, the ESM, like the Lisbon Agenda, would offer great opportunities to promote and facilitate integration in social policy on account of its ambiguity (Borrás and Radaelli 2011). At first glance, this is exactly how both the Lisbon Agenda and EU 2020 presented the ESM. Each provided statements of intent backed up by benchmarks that remained in part aspirational and in part tangible. The extensive use of guiding principles or 'soft law' had the potential to promote integration through deliberation. The function of the ESM should have been to stimulate this form of integration.

But to understand functionalist integration, we need to have a clearer understanding of what a functionalist integration would involve. An effective functionalist analysis must identify both the consequences of a given pattern of social relations for the system and an examination of the conditions that make these consequences functional (Bredemeier 1955, 178). Beneath, we pursue a functionalist analysis of the ESM's role in the EU's main mechanisms of economic governance since 2000. Our aim is to examine first how the ESM has been used to generate processes that led to European integration, and second to reveal under what conditions these integrative processes led to greater integration.

Bredemeier offers us six key characteristics of a 'productive' (that is, effective) functionalist analysis that we can use to demonstrate how functionalist arguments linked the ESM to the system of European governance as they changed in relation to austerity measures. For reasons of space, Bredemeier's procedure will be stated before illustrating how the ESM contributed to functionalist discourses in relation to the EU 2020 (for more detail on the Lisbon Agenda see Dannreuther 2006) and in specific relation to Social Investment Programmes. The aim of this analysis is to examine what the consequences are of the ESM and what the conditions are that make these consequences functional.

(1) Productive analysis begins with a statement of the kind of action necessary to maintain some system of inter-relationships, namely, the system of which the observed uniformity is a part. (Bredemeier 1955, 180)

The ESM maintains two economic systems. The first is the EU's as it offers mechanisms for alleviating the costs of economic integration. There is a broad political and academic consensus that national welfare systems prevail in the management of domestic political economies (Esping Anderson 1990; Hall and Soskice 2001; Thelen 2004). The ESM complements these but does so through an explicit asymmetry between economic and social rights and objectives (Scharpf 2002; Dannreuther 2006). The second system that the ESM sustains is the global capitalist system. Under the Lisbon Agenda, the ESM was presented as the EU's response to globalisation, explicitly differentiating the EU from other global economies through its social inclusion and through more democratically accountable methods of open methods of governance and coordination. The EU2020 agenda emphasised that a socially orientated response to the financial crisis would be led at the EU level while also implying that the ESM would contribute to sustaining Europe's social economy.

(2) It states the motivational conditions which are necessary to produce that action (the normative criteria of gratification which will yield the relevant action). (Bredemeier 1955, 180)

Do member states pursue aspects of the ESM to realise better societies in Europe? Or do they try to comply so that they look like good Europeans keen to strengthen the union between the member states? The motivational conditions for the effective realisation of an ESM have changed dramatically from the post-Cold War optimism that informed the Maastricht model to fire-fighting responses to the sovereign debt crisis. During the 1990s, the reuniting of Europe rejected the bipolar world view of the Cold War, and sought instead to pursue 'third way' political agendas based on good governance, social democracy and social inclusion (Painter 2000). The motivations were still for economic growth, but through more consensual processes such as the Open Method of Coordination, established in the 1997 European Employment Strategy and guided by principles of Good Governance, set out in the Commission's 2002 'Good Governance' White Paper. These were developed in subsequent proposals from the Commission (Commission 2007a, 2007b, 2007c, 2008, 2012; Mosher and Trubek 2003).

After the sovereign debt crisis, a quite different set of concerns motivated the decision-makers of the EU. To be allowed to deliver national social and labour policies, national economic policies now had to focus on bond market evaluations, and also, if required, the judgements of the 'Troika' of the Commission, the European Central Bank and the International Monetary Fund (Achtsioglou and Doherty 2014). Policy interventions have been more focused on limiting unemployment, reducing tax on companies and trying to capture the growth in informal employment (Commission 2012). The Commission's repeated emphasis on member state compliance with National Reform programmes despite their social costs demonstrates that member states have sought to support the realisation of EU2020 goals and the EU as a system, rather than creating a better society for Europe.

(3) It describes the motivational patterns actually operating so as to produce the uniformity under analysis. (Bredemeier 1955, 180)

In the period between Maastricht and austerity, the Lisbon Agenda played an important role in promoting individualistic social risk management policies in place of collective ones (Dannreuther 2006). These included seeing welfare as a social investment, confirming individual responsibility, and presenting the possibilities of welfare as contingent on prevailing economic conditions (Ellison and Fenger 2013). During the 2000s when there was significant credit availability in many of the EU's economies, when the global economic system was expanding under continued growth, and while the EU was able to locate itself as a service provider to this, the motivation of member states to work towards an ESM based on services and the knowledge-based economy was strong. Under the austerity of Europe 2020, the same motivational criteria of self-sufficiency and resilience remain. But the broader macroeconomic demand that kept both smaller businesses and flexible work patterns solvent, and the availability of public sector support have gone.

The ESM was therefore integrated into the political economy of the EU in two ways. First, the Lisbon Agenda did not promote open and socially inclusive strategies across the EU as the ESM implied. There were successes in the access of women to the labour market, but this access was often realised by introducing less favourable conditions for women. As the economy contracted after 2008, it became clear that the recession hit women's jobs more aggressively than men's (Rubery and Rafferty 2013). The actual motivation of the ESM was less about raising standards of living or work than about lowering them. The second explanation was that the Open Method of Coordination (OMC) introduced through the ESM, normalised under the Lisbon Agenda and adapted into the semester system by the EU 2020 agenda, greatly empowered core executives (Borrás and Peters 2011). While the Commission may have benefitted in the initial design of the OMC, later reforms were dominated by the member states (de la Porte 2011). So, the ESM contributed to less rather than more social influence on EU policy-making. Certainly, labour market policies to promote flexicurity led to greater control by increasingly influential and isolated political elites (Gwiazda 2011), rather than its decentralisation to social partners.

(4) [A functionalist analysis] seeks to find the source of those patterns (to isolate the normative criteria responsible for the observed actions). (Bredemeier 1955, 180)

Activities designed to promote and sustain the ESM were therefore concerned with the Commission's agenda. Many of the changes to social policy in national administrations were brought through by national governments and in accordance with domestic political agendas, such as those associated with the Third Way (Keman 2011). If anything the ESM, and the broader governance mechanisms of the Lisbon Agenda and EU 2020 that it supported, undermined the significance of the very groups that the ESM was intended to privilege. EU actors and civil society have become far less influential than implied in the initial ambition of the OMC (Hyman 2005); the ECB's macroeconomic agenda has presented a powerful constraint on any social agenda that might lead to broader economic stimulus, and at the national level governments have been able to deploy austerity arguments from the EU-level macroeconomic agenda to discipline domestic labour markets. Troika-type reforms have been damaging across a wide range of policy areas (e.g. Ladi and Tsarouhas 2014), and have had a devastating impact on the institutional and real experience of people across Europe, leading one group of commentators to argue that '... if the path of economic austerity, despite all opposition, is maintained until 2014/2015 and then experiences a new upswing the policy disaster for European social democracy and the trade unions will be complete' (Busch et al. 2013, 1). In southern Europe, other commentators have warned that the political cost of austerity has been a 'politics without choices' that could destabilise the South of Europe (Bosco and Verney 2012).

But while the reforms associated with post-crisis austerity were indeed damaging, they were not innovative. Social Investment Programmes (SIP) were well established many years before the financial crisis began (e.g. Jenson and Saint Martin 2003). The mechanism of social investment was a global phenomenon that provided a greater role for the state, an extension of citizenship to capture marginalised groups and the decentralisation of governance practices to communities (Jenson 2009). SIPs introduced new practices of asset-based welfare and community-led finance initiatives to deliver better quality welfare (Prabhakar 2013; Ridge 2013). These reforms drew on evidence-based policies to better capture the performance of policy, to identify where support was needed and to disseminate good practice. They replaced traditional methods of social protection by enabling individual emancipation, but in return for more explicit reciprocal social contracts (Cantillon and van Lancker 2013); and they challenged the dominance of national compromises, revealing how national compromises were not isolated from European agendas and were also not just national (Schelkle 2012).

> (5) It compares the consequences of the operating motivation with the motivations described as necessary, including the deviant modes of adjusting to frustration of the efforts to meet the criteria in question. (Bredemeier 1955, 180)

There have been significant consequences arising from following the ESM both as a project and as an ill-specified ideal type. At the policy level, the ESM with its promotion of social investment policies (SIP) has contributed to a growth of such policies across countries and policy areas over the last 20 years (Van Kersbergen and Hemerijck 2012). SIPs have offered a dynamic and innovative response to what have been seen as foot-dragging by conceptually and politically intransigent welfare states (Ewert and Evers 2014). But during this period, inequality has increased dramatically in relation to mid-twentieth-century levels, while class and social stratification remain powerful predictors of SIP performance (Pintelon et al. 2013). Others have identified that the SIP agenda has increased since the onset of austerity, and that although this may demonstrate a consistency in welfare reform, the practice of these reforms diverges in member state and local contexts, with the countries least likely to deliver social investment also being those most in need of social investment (Kvist 2013).

Pursuing an ESM through SIPs may appear to offer universal and innovative solutions, but it may also enable the persistence of enduring forms of inequality across the EU.

This is in part due to the lack of conceptual clarity of social investment. It is difficult to differentiate, for example, between investments made for social purposes (to address uncertainties in life such as disability) and those made for economic purposes (to improve access to the labour market through skills training) (Nolan 2013). Differences in language and interpretation contribute to confusion in debates over welfare policy (Béland 2011). So while SIPs may not have led to dramatic cuts in welfare expenditure, they have led to a greater subordination of workers to market forces without radically reducing stubbornly high poverty rates (Vandenbroucke and Vleminckx 2011).

This lack of clear evidence that the ESM has transferred real benefits via SIP, especially to those countries undergoing austerity-driven reforms, and also exacerbates a political problem for welfare reform. One consequence of the devastating effect that austerity has had on welfare states has been the finding that while some political parties are sanctioned by voters for welfare state retrenchment, many voters also value economic stability. Only supporters of welfare states who believe that welfare states do not harm economic growth will punish parties who impose welfare state reforms (Giger and Nelson 2013). In other words, support for the ESM, and its assumption that competitiveness and social justice are 'two sides of the same coin', becomes an electoral liability for national politicians trying to comply with National Reform Programmes. The ESM could even have contributed to delivering votes to the right of the political spectrum as seen in the 2014 EP elections.

(6) It finally assesses the role played by the uniformity in question in contributing to the system of which it is a part. (Bredemeier 1955, 180)

The last of Bredemeier's recommendations encourages us to reflect on how the ESM has contributed overall to the EU as a system and to global capitalism. Treating the ESM as an 'ideal type', analysts could use it to differentiate between the European economy and the rest of the world. But because the ESM was also used in the Lisbon Agenda to coordinate collective responses to globalisation, and in the process helped to redefine welfare as social investment, we should also interrogate the values that it selected as European, and consider what these values mean for the reality of society in Europe.

First, the ESM only offers the potential for politically motivated social justice rather than juridical entitlements. This dramatically weakens the argument for any kind of ESM at the European level, and for seeking to sustain higher levels of rights for European workers over others in the global economy. The ESM needs to be part of a universal commitment to international labour standards and, if Europe is to claim any legitimacy for having higher labour standards, the EU should be more aggressive in enforcing international standards through recourse to the law.

Second, the motivations for an ESM are orientated more to the realisation of the EU and its survival as a system rather than the improvement of Europe's society. This may have its roots in the optimism of post-Cold War reintegration. But, the ESM has now confirmed not just the subordinate position of workers in the EU, but also that welfare is subordinate to the market. The sources of these changes have been both endogenous, in the social democratic reform agenda that has characterised EU policies since Lisbon, and exogenous, in that the growth in financial markets has contained the scope of welfare expenditure.

Conclusion

The use of Bredemeier's model of functionalist analysis has allowed us to expose and explain the inadequacies of the ESM in the context of the overall transformation of EU values, policies and governance in the 22 years since the Maastricht Treaty. In particular, the analysis has pointed up the *dysfunctionality* of the ESM under the impact of the Lisbon Agenda and EU2020.

What is less explicable is why the ESM was not more ambitious then, and indeed now, when faced with pressing social challenges (e.g. IFRC 2013). Why has it not been called upon to define basic standards for the world's richest economy that include, for example, maintaining children's health, providing jobs, ensuring a living wage, linking pay to directors' salaries, setting a standard poverty rate across the EU and a wide range of other benchmarks for basic social outcomes? Moreover, such standards could have offered far more progressive alternatives for radical reform which could have been placed before European electorates. The conflict between the motivations for the EU as a political system remain in stark contrast to any recognisably effective practice of social security, and this gap has been filled by innovative social investment policies. Whatever the long-term effect of SIPs may be, in the meantime they have interpolated similar values of public value, individualisation of risk and market hegemony that the corporate sector has experienced under financialisation (Froud et al. 2000).

From a functionalist standpoint, the consequences of the ESM have been to introduce a poor alternative to national welfare systems, always subordinated to monetarist policies. In the context of the recent crisis, they enabled the removal of social protection from the market, and its substitution by social investment for the market. The ESM and the conditions under which it was introduced have changed dramatically. If it is to continue to support rather than undermine the values and functionality of the EU, it needs to change.

Acknowledgements

This paper benefitted from comments on an earlier draft from Dagmar Schiek, Hugo Radice, reviewers for this journal and colleagues at the University of Leeds.

References

Achtsioglou, E., and M. Doherty. 2014. "There Must Be Some Way Out of Here." *European Law Journal* 20 (2): 219–240.
Aglietta, M. 2012. "The European Vortex." *New Left Review* 75 (May–June): 15–36.
Auer, P. 2010. "What's in a Name? The Rise (and Fall?) of Flexicurity." *Journal of Industrial Relations* 52 (3): 371–386.
Azmanova, A. 2009. "1989 and the European Social Model Transition Without Emancipation?" *Philosophy & Social Criticism* 35 (9): 1019–1037.
Becker, Uwe. 2007. "Open Systemness and Contested Reference Frames and Change." *Socio-Economic Review* 5 (2): 261–286.
Becker, Uwe. 2009. *Open Varieties of Capitalism: Continuity, Change and Performance*. London: Palgrave Macmillan.
Béland, Daniel. 2011. "The Politics of Social Policy Language." *Social Policy & Administration* 45 (1): 1–18.
Borrás, Susana, and B. Guy Peters. 2011. "The Lisbon Strategy's Empowerment of Core Executives." *Journal of European Public Policy* 18 (4): 525–545.
Borrás, Susana, and Claudio M. Radaelli. 2011. "The Politics of Governance Architectures." *Journal of European Public Policy* 18 (4): 463–484.

Bosco, Anna, and Susannah Verney. 2012. "Electoral Epidemic: The Political Cost of Economic Crisis in Southern Europe, 2010–2011." *South European Society and Politics* 17 (2): 129–154.

Bredemeier, H. C. 1955. "The Methodology of Functionalism." *American Sociological Review* 20 (2): 173–180.

Busch, Klaus, Christoph Hermann, Karl Hinrichs, and Thorsten Schulten. 2013. *Euro Crisis, Austerity Policy and The European Social Model*. Berlin: European Economic and Social Policy Friedrich-Ebert-Stiftung.

Cantillon, Bea, and Wim Van Lancker. 2013. "Three Shortcomings of the Social Investment Perspective." *Social Policy and Society* 12: 533–564.

Collier, David, Jody La Porte, and Jason Seawright. 2012. "Putting Typologies to Work." *Political Research Quarterly* 65 (1): 217–232.

Commission. 1994. "European Social Policy – A Way Forward For The Union." COM (94) 333 final Brussels. 27.07.1994.

Commission. 2007a. "Opportunities, Access and Solidarity: Towards a New Social Vision for 21st Century Europe." COM2007 726, 20.11.2007.

Commission. 2007b. "Social Reality Stocktaking: Interim Report to the 2007 Spring European Council." COM2007 63 final Brussels, 26.2.2007.

Commission. 2007c. *Report on the Public Consultation on Europe's Social Reality and on a New Social Vision for 21st Century Europe*. Staff Working Paper.

Commission. 2008. "Renewed Social Agenda: Opportunities, Access and Solidarity in 21st Century Europe." COM2008 412 final Brussels, 2.7.2008.

Commission. 2012. "Towards a Job-Rich Recovery." COM/2012/0173 final.

Copeland, P. 2012. "EU Enlargement, the Clash of Capitalisms and the European Social Model." *Comparative European Politics* 10 (4): 476–504.

Dannreuther, C. 2006. "Regulation Theory and the EU." *Competition and Change* 10 (2): 180–199.

de la Porte, Caroline. 2011. "Principal–agent theory and the Open Method of Co-ordination." *Journal of European Public Policy* 18 (4): 485–503.

Deutsch, Karl W., Sidney A. Burrell, Robert A. Kann, Maurice Lee, Jr., Martin Lichterman, Raymond E. Lindgren, Francis L. Loewenheim, and Richard W. Van Wagenen. 1957. *Political Community and the North Atlantic Area*. Princeton: Princeton University Press.

Ellison, Marion, and Menno Fenger. 2013. "Introduction: 'New' Welfare in Practice: Trends, Challenges and Dilemmas." *Social Policy and Society* 12 (4): 547–552.

Elman, Colin. 2005. "Explanatory Typologies in Qualitative Studies of International Politics." *International Organization* 59 (2): 293–326.

Esping Andersen, Gøsta. 1990. *The Three Worlds of Welfare Capitalism*. Cambridge: Polity.

Ewert, Benjamin, and Adalbert Evers. 2014. "Blueprints for the Future of Welfare Provision?" *Social Policy and Society* 1–10. doi:10.1017/S1474746414000074

Forsberg, T. 2011. "Normative Power Europe, Once Again: A Conceptual Analysis of an Ideal Type." *Journal of Common Market Studies* 49 (6): 1183–1204.

Froud, Julie, Colin Haslam, Sukhdev Johal, and Karel Williams. 2000. "Shareholder Value and Financialization: Consultancy Promises, Management Moves." *Economy and Society* 29 (1): 80–110.

Geras, N. 1971. "Essence and Appearance: Aspects of Fetishism in Marx's Capital." *New Left Review* 65: 69–85.

Gerth, H. H., and C. Wright Mills. 2009. "The Man and his Work." In *Essays in Sociology*, edited by M. Weber. London: Routledge.

Giger, Nathalie, and Moira Nelson. 2013. "The Welfare State or the Economy?" *European Sociological Review* 29 (5): 1083–1094.

Gwiazda, Anna. 2011. "The Europeanization of Flexicurity: The Lisbon Strategy's Impact on Employment Policies in Italy and Poland." *Journal of European Public Policy* 18 (4): 546–565.

Haas, E. 1958. *The Uniting of Europe: Political, Social and Economic Forces, 1950—1957*. Stanford: Stanford University Press.

Hall, Peter A., and David Soskice, eds. 2001. *Varieties of Capitalism*. Oxford: OUP.

Hancké, Bob, Martin Rhodes, and Mark Thatcher, eds. 2008. *Beyond Varieties of Capitalism*. Oxford: Oxford UP.

Hemerijck, Anton. 2002. "The Self-Transformation of the European Social Model(s)." In *Why We Need a New Welfare State*, edited by Gøsta Esping-Andersen. Oxford: OUP.

Hyman, R. 2005. "Trade Unions and the Politics of the European Social Model." *Economic and Industrial Democracy* 26 (1): 9–40.

IFRC. 2013. "Think Differently Humanitarian Impacts of the Economic Crisis in Europe." Accessed March 7. http://www.ifrc.org/PageFiles/134339/1260300-Economic%20crisis%20Report_EN_LR.pdf

Jenson, Jane. 2009. "Lost in Translation: The Social Investment Perspective and Gender Equality." *Social Politics* 16 (4): 446–483.

Jenson, Jane, and Denis Saint-Martin. 2003. "New Routes to Social Cohesion? Citizenship and the Social Investment State." *The Canadian Journal of Sociology* 28 (1): 77–99.

Jepsen, M., and Pascual. 2005. "The European Social Model: An Exercise in Deconstruction." *Journal of European Social Policy* 15 (3): 231–245.

Jessop, B. 2010. "Cultural Political Economy and Critical Policy Studies." *Critical Policy Studies* 3 (3–4): 336–356.

Jessop, B., Brigitte Young, and Christoph Scherrer, eds. 2014. *Cultures of Finance and Crisis Dynamics*. London: Routledge.

Keman, H. 2011. "Third Ways and Social Democracy: The Right Way to Go?" *British Journal of Political Science* 41 (3): 671–680.

Kvist, Jon. 2013. "The Post-Crisis European Social Model: Developing or Dismantling Social Investments?" *Journal of International and Comparative Social Policy* 29 (1): 91–107.

Ladi, Stella, and Dimitris Tsarouhas. 2014. "The Politics of Austerity and Public Policy Reform in the EU." *Political Studies Review* 12 (2): 171–180.

Lapavitsas, C., A. Kaltenbrunner, G. Labrinidis, D. Lindo, J. Meadway, J. Michell, J. P. Painceira, E. Pires, J. Powell, A. Stenfors, N. Teles, and L. Vatikiotis. 2012. *Crisis in the Eurozone*. London: Verso.

Montanari, Ingalill, Kenneth Nelson, and Joakim Palme. 2008. "Towards a European Social Model? Trends in Social Insurance Among EU Countries 1980–2000." *European Societies* 10 (5): 787–810.

Mosher, J., and D. Trubek. 2003. "Alternative Approaches to Governance in the EU: EU Social Policy and the European Employment Strategy." *Journal of Common Market Studies* 41 (1): 63–88.

Nolan, B. 2013. "What Use is 'Social Investment'?" *Journal of European Social Policy* 23 (5): 459–468.

Oxford Dictionary. 2014. "Heuristic Device." Accessed June 11. http://www.oxfordreference.com/view/10.1093/acref/9780199533008.001.0001/acref-9780199533008-e-1001

Painter, J. 2000. "A Third Way for Europe? Discourse, Regulation and the European Question in Britain." *Tijdschrift Voor Economische En Sociale Geografie* 91 (3): 227–236.

Pintelon, Olivier, Bea Cantillon, Karel Van den Bosch, and Christopher T. Whelan. 2013. "The Social Stratification of Social Risks: The Relevance of Class for Social Investment Strategies." *Journal of European Social Policy* 23 (1): 52–67.

Prabhakar, R. 2013. "Asset-Based Welfare: Financialization or Financial Inclusion?" *Critical Social Policy* 33 (4): 658–678.

Ridge, T. 2013. "'We are All in This Together'? The Hidden Costs of Poverty, Recession and Austerity Policies on Britain's Poorest Children." *Children & Society* 27 (5): 406–417.

Rogowski, R. 2009. *The European Social Model and Transitional Labour Markets*. London: Ashgate.

Rosamond, B. 2014. "Three Ways of Speaking Europe to the World: Markets, Peace, Cosmopolitan Duty and the EU's Normative Power." *British Journal of Politics and International Relations* 16 (1): 133–148.

Rubery, J., and A. Rafferty. 2013. "Women and Recession Revisited." *Work, Employment and Society* 273: 414–432.

Scharpf, F. 2002. "The European Social Model: Coping with the Challenges of Diversity." *Journal of Common Market Studies* 40 (4): 645–670.

Schelkle, Waltraud. 2012. "Collapsing Worlds and Varieties of welfare capitalism: In Search of a New Political Economy of Welfare." LEQS Paper No. 54/2012. Accessed April 22, 2014. www.lse.ac.uk/europeanInstitute/LEQS/LEQSPaper54.pdf

Smismans, Stijn. 2011. "From Harmonization to Co-ordination? EU Law in the Lisbon Governance Architecture." *Journal of European Public Policy* 18 (4): 504–524.

Stone Sweet, A., and W. Sandholtz. 1997. "European Integration and Supranational Governance." *Journal of European Public Policy* 4 (3): 297–317.

Stout, Margaret. 2010. "Revisiting the (Lost) Art of Ideal-Typing in Public Administration." *Administrative Theory & Praxis* 32 (4): 491–519.

ter Haar, Beryl, and Paul Copeland. 2010. "What are the Future Prospects for the European Social Model? An Analysis of EU Equal Opportunities and Employment Policy." *European Law Journal* 16 (3): 273–291.

Thelen, K. 2004. *How Institutions Evolve: The Political Economy of Skills in Germany, Britain, the United States, and Japan*. Cambridge: Cambridge University Press.

Tranholm-Mikkelsen, J. 1991. "Neofunctionalism: Obstinate or Obsolete?" *Millennium: Journal of International Studies* 20 (1): 1–22.

van Apeldoorn, Bastiaan, and Sandy Hager. 2010. "The Social Purpose of New Governance: Lisbon and the Limits to Legitimacy." *Journal of International Relations and Development* 13 (3): 209–238.

Van Kersbergen, Kees, and Anton Hemerijck. 2012. "Two Decades of Change in Europe: The Emergence of the Social Investment State." *Journal of Social Policy* 41: 475–492.

Vandenbroucke, Frank, and Koen Vleminckx. 2011. "Disappointing Poverty Trends: Is the Social Investment State to Blame?" *Journal of European Social Policy* 21 (5): 450–471.

Weber, M. 1949. "The Methodology of the Social Sciences." Accessed June 5, 20114. https://archive.org/stream/maxweberonmethod00webe#page/91/mode/1up

Zielonka. 2014. *Is the EU Doomed?* Cambridge: Polity Press.

Index

Abs, Herman-Josef 39
actual output 76
Adenauer, Konrad 40
anti-EU political movements 86
asymmetrically interconnected economic
    spaces 5
Atlantic Fordism 5, 6
austerity measures enforced after Eurozone
    crisis 32–33, 74–82, 92
authoritarian constitutionalism 12
authoritarian neoliberalism 12
authoritarian statism 12

bailout agreements for the Eurozone
    crisis 1, 11, 62, 63, 66–68, 70
banking union 36–37, 62, 68–70
Bank of England 79, 80
Bank of International Settlements (BIS) 64
Barroso, José Manuel 65
Basel 1 framework 65
Basel 2 framework 65
Basel II accord 61
Becker, Uwe 2, 3
Big Bazooka 63
Bofinger, Peter 37
Bredemeier's model of functionalist
    analysis 89–94
business freedom 24

capitalism: comparative 4; corporatist 22,
    26–29; embedded 23–29; empirical case
    21–22; heterogeneity in Europe 17–30;
    ideal types of 21, 87; influencing economic
    policies 2; institutional diversity of 21–23;
    liberal 22, 25–26; regulated 5; typologies of
    21–23; varieties of 4
capital-labour relationship 22, 24
China's co-dependence with USA 5
Coalition Agreement of 2013 34, 35
community method of integration 5
comparative capitalism (CC) 4
comparative cognitive mapping (CCM)
    45, 48–49
competitiveness: gap in EU countries 21;
    improving by Ordnungspolitik 33–34;
    not needing a social policy 39–40

compossible VoC 4, 6
corporatist capitalism 22, 26–29
corruption 23–25, 27
Covered Bond Purchase Programme (CBPP1)
    62–63
crisis management: crises of 11–13; strategy 8
current account deficits of Eurozone
    countries 18
Cyprus' economic crisis 12

Dannreuther, Charles 2
das deutsche Modell 7–8
das Modell Deutschland 5–8, 40; dominance
    of 10, 13
debt brake 11, 34, 35, 51
debt-default-deflation dynamics 10, 13
depoliticisation 75, 78–82
Deutsche Mark zone 9
diagnostic ideas 46
die Wende 8
Dillow, Chris 77
disciplinary neoliberalism 80
discursive convergence 2
Dombert, Andreas 66
Draghi, Mario 35, 63, 69

economic convergence 6, 8–10, 17
economic heterogeneity of EU members 29
economic imbalances between EU member
    states 1
economic policy ideas changing 46–49
Economic Protection Legislation (EPL)
    23–25
economic space: European 5–7; variegated 4–6,
    13–14
economic stimulation 46
embedded capitalism 22, 26–29; movement
    between liberal and 23–26
embedded economies between corporatist and
    patrimonial varieties 2
embourgeoisement of the workers 81
empirical case capitalism 21–22
employment protection 24–25
employment structure of EU countries 19
Erhard, Ludwig 34, 35, 39–40
Estonia's exports 19

EU: economic and monetary union of 8–9; economic governance of 11–14; economics 7–10; economies 1; increased integration of states 7–8; reform of 85
EU2020 89–91
Eucken, Walter 35, 36
Euro: saving 34; as a world currency 9
European Banking Authority (EBA) 65
European Central Bank (ECB) 1, 2, 9, 12, 35, 36, 44, 46, 50–54, 59–71, 74, 79
European Coal and Steel Community (ECSC) 5
European Commission 1; enforcing austerity 74–82
European Court of Justice (ECJ) 74
European Economic and Monetary Union (EMU) 2, 9, 11, 45, 50–53; handling crisis 66, 68–70; pre-crisis policy principles 60–62; preventing collapse of 59–71
European economic and political spaces 5–7
European Economic Community (EEC) 5
European Financial Stabilisation Mechanism (EFSM) 11
European Financial Stability Facility (EFSF) 11, 65, 67
European Insurance and Occupational Pensions Authority (EIOPA) 65
European Roundtable of Industrialists 9
European Securities and Markets Authority (ESMA) 65
European Social Model (ESM): different components of 88; and its relevancy 86–94; and the mythology of functionalism 89–93
European sovereign debt crisis 1
European Stability Mechanism (ESM) 2, 11–12, 64, 67
European Systemic Risk Board (ESRB) 65
European Union. *See* EU
Eurosclerosis 6
Eurozone crisis 10–11; management of by the European Central Bank (ECB) 59–71
exports of EU countries 19–20
export specialisation of EU countries 19–20
extend and pretend policies 11, 13

financial freedom 24
financialisation 1
financial regulation policy 61
Finland's innovation capacity 21
Fiscal Compact 2, 11–12
fiscal consolidation of indebted countries 32–33
fiscal discipline as a fiscal policy 61
fiscal freedom 24
Fiscal Pact 74–75
fiscal union 62, 66–67
Fordism. *See* Atlantic Fordism
France: exposed to European peripheral banking systems 69–70; pressures during Eurozone crisis 48
Francis, Pope 41
freedom from corruption 24

free market 80–81
Freiburg School 34
functionalism and the European Social Model (ESM) 89–93
functionalist integration 89

German Bundesbank 33–36
German Council of Economic Advisors 37
Germanic Europe 9
Germany: advocating bailout agreement 62; advocating Ordoliberalism 32–41; asymmetrical interdependence with other EU economies 7–10; capitalism 2, 7–8; changing its position on crisis management strategy 68–70; exports of 7–8; exposed to European peripheral banking systems 69–70; giving concessions for Eurozone crisis 66–68; innovation capacity 21; neo-mercantilist foreign economic policy 7–8; overcoming its World War II debts 38–39; pressures during Eurozone crisis 47–48; response to economic crisis 11–12; shaping the structure of the EMU 59
GIPSI countries 32
governance by ideal type 86–89
Great Moderation (1990's) 9
Greece: bailout agreements 67; economic crisis in 12; employment structure 19; exports 19; level of embedded capitalism 29
Grexit 12

Hartz labour market reforms 8
Heinemann, Frank 36
Hellwig, Martin 36
heterogeneity of European capitalisms 2
Horn, Gustav 37

ideal types of governance 86–87
ideal-typical capitalism 21
ideational convergence 47–49
Independent High Level Group on Financial Supervision 65
Index of Economic Freedom (IEF) 23–25
individualistic social risk management policies 91
Institute for New Economic Thinking (INET) 37
instrumental ideas 46
International Monetary Fund 1
intra-European transfer of resources and risks 61
Ireland's exports 19
Italy: impacting German and French banks 69–70; level of embedded capitalism 29

Jessop, Bob 2
Juncker, Jean-Claude 69

Keynesianiansim 34–37
Keynesian outlook: expressed by Christian Noyer 53–55; expressed by Nicolas Sarkozy 52–53; as proposed solution to Eurozone crisis 46

Krämer, Walter 36
Krampf, Arie 2

Lammert, Norbert 37
Larosière, Jacques de 65
Les économistes atterrés 76
liberal capitalism 22, 25–26; movement
    between embedded and 23–26
liberal interventionism 39–40
Lisbon Agenda 89–91
Lisbon Treaty 61
London Debt Agreement 38–39
long-term refinancing operation (LTRO) 63–64

Maastricht Treaty 36, 40, 78
Macroprudential Research Network (MaRs) 65
macro-prudential financial policy 64–65
Martin, Bill 77
Merkel, Angela 36, 37, 40, 44, 45, 66–69;
    evidence of Ordoliberal outlook 47–50, 55
Merkel method 11
Milan Summit (1985) 6
mode of social regulation (MSR) 87
monetary and fiscal authorities as a monetary
    policy 60–61
Monnet method of integration 5, 6
Müller-Armack, Alfred 38
mutualizing Eurozone debts 36–37

negative integration 7
neo-corporatist foreign economic policy 8
neofunctionalism 89
neoliberalism 2, 6, 12–13; adjustments in *das
    Modell Deutschland* 8
neo-mercantilist foreign economic policy of
    Germany 7–8
Netherlands' exports 19
new constitutionalism 80
no bailout clause 61, 67
normal capacity utilisation 78
North Atlantic Financial Crisis (NAFC) 10
Northern Eurozone members 17, 19, 29; current
    account surplus 32–33
Noyer, Christian 45, 53–55

OECD on measuring output gap 76–77
Office for Budget Responsibility (OBR)
    (British) 76–77
Open Method of Coordination (OMC) 7, 90, 91
Ordnungspolitik 33–35, 38–41
Ordoliberalism 2, 6; expressed by Angela
    Merkel 47–50; expressed by Axel Weber
    50–52; expressed by Christian Noyer 53–55;
    expressed by Nicolas Sarkozy 52–53;
    inability to solve the Eurozone crisis 32–41;
    proposed solution to Eurozone crisis 45–46
output gap (OG) 76–78
outright monetary transactions (OMTs) program
    35, 36, 64

patrimonial capitalism 22, 26–29
PIIGS 10
policy ideas change and convergence 46–48
political democracy 81
political economy 22, 25–26
Portugal: employment structure 19; exports 19
potential output 76
price stability 51, 63; primacy of 35, 45–46
principled ideas 46
principle of mutual recognition 6
productive potential 77
productivity pessimism 77–78
Product Market Regulation (PMR) 23–25

Radice, Hugo 2
Red-Green Coalition (1998–2005) 8
re-exports 19
regulated capitalism 5
Regulation Approach (RA) 87
regulatory responses to financial crisis 1
Rhenish model of capitalism 5, 37–38
risk sharing to handle the Eurozone crisis 59

Sarkozy, Nicolas 45, 48; Keynesian and
    Ordoliberal outlooks 52–53, 55
Schäuble, Wolfgang 33, 36, 66, 69
Schiller, Karl 40
Schröder, Gerhard 40
Securities Markets Programme (SMP) 63
single resolution mechanism (SRM) 66, 71
single supervision mechanism (SSM) 66,
    68, 71
Sinn, Hans-Werner 34, 36, 37
Slovakia: exports 19; level of embedded
    capitalism 29
Social Democratic Party (SPD) 7–8, 34, 35
social forms of learning 47
Social Investment Programmes (SIP) 92
Social Liberal Coalition 8
Social Market Economy (German) 2
social policy for market competition 39–40
Soros, George 37
Southern Eurozone members 17, 19, 29;
    indebted 32–33
Soziale Marktwirtschaft 34, 38–41
space economies 4
Spain: bailout agreement 68; exports 19;
    impacting German and French banks 69–70
spare productive capacity 77
Stability and Growth Pact 8–9, 11, 36, 45, 61,
    75, 79
Stark, Jürgen 35, 60
state control of economy 24
statist liberalism 22, 26–29
structural deficit (SD) 75–82; economics of
    75–78; as a policy target 2; and the politics
    of depoliticisation 78–82
sub-prime mortgage market crisis 1
Sweden's innovation capacity 21

threat-rigidity thesis 47
*Toward a Genuine Economic and Monetary
    Union* 69
trade freedom 24
Treaty of Rome 5
Treaty on Stability, Coordination and
    Governance (TSCG) 11, 74–75, 79, 85
Trichet, J.-C. 62, 63
Tripartite Commission on the German
    Debt 38
Troika 1, 12

union method of crisis management
    11–13
USA's co-dependence with China 5

Van Esch, Femke 2
Van Rompuy, Herman 69
variegated economic space 4–6, 13–14
varieties of capitalism (VoC) 4
Varoufakis, Yannis 9

Weber, Axel 45, 50–52
Weidmann, Jens 35
welfare systems, national 90–93
WG1 on The New Global Finance 1
WG3 on Regulatory Responses 1
Wirtschaftswunder 38
Worldwide Governance Indicators (WGI) 23, 26–28

Young, Brigitte 2

For Product Safety Concerns and Information please contact our EU representative GPSR@taylorandfrancis.com Taylor & Francis Verlag GmbH, Kaufingerstraße 24, 80331 München, Germany

Batch number: 08153807

Printed by Printforce, the Netherlands